BIBLICAL BELIEFS

Doctrines

Believers Should

Know

Evangelical Training Association

110 Bridge Street • Box 327

Wheaton, IL 60189-0327

Cover Design: Kurtz Design Studio, Tulsa, OK

2001 Edition, Second Printing

ISBN: 0-910566-10-0

CONTENTS

Inspiration of the Bible

The inspiration of the Bible is of great importance, for all Christian doctrines are developed from the Bible and rest upon it for authority. The conviction that the eternal God has revealed himself to man has always been central in the Christian faith. Since man could never have discovered God by himself, Christians have always held that God makes himself known to man supernaturally. The books which form the canon of the Old and New Testaments as originally written are fully inspired and entirely free from error. These books constitute the written Word of God, the only infallible rule of faith and practice.

To accept the inspiration of the Bible does not mean that every passage can be explained or understood. There are depths in God's Book that the mind of man cannot fathom, but far from being indications of weakness or failure, they serve to prove the Bible's divine origin. If the intelligence of man could master the Bible from beginning to end, it might be justifiable to question its divine origin. God has revealed a sufficient knowledge of his love and grace for believers to have both faith and hope in him, and be assured that "if any man will do his will, he shall know of the doctrine" (John 7:17). If Christians study the Bible, not with prejudice and criticism, but with faith in and love for its author, they will understand its message.

There is a distinction between revelation and inspiration. Revelation is the record of God's communication through men. Inspiration is God's power enabling man to record correctly the truth revealed. The word *inspiration*, used only twice in the Bible (Job 32:8; II Tim. 3:16), means the "inbreathing" of God into man so that man spoke or wrote God's revelation of truth with authority and accuracy (II Pet. 1:21).

All that is in the Bible has not been directly revealed to men. The Bible contains history in the language of men, even of wicked men, but there is no part that is not inspired. The Spirit so directed and influenced the writers that they were kept from any error of fact or doctrine.

Inspiration does not mean God has given his approval to every recorded statement. The Bible records the lies of Satan (for example, "Thou shall not surely die"), and the misdeeds of many wicked people, some of whom God used to communicate his message. For example, the book of Job contains the truths of Jehovah, the words of Satan, the speech of Elihu, and the arguments of Job and the three friends. Satan, Job, and his three friends did not speak by inspiration of God. They spoke their own opinions. Inspiration means that no one of them is misrepresented, but that each one spoke the words attributed to him in Scripture. The fact that misdeeds like Saul's slaughter of the priests, David's numbering of the people, and Herod's massacre of the innocents are recorded in the Bible, does not imply that God approved of them, but the divine record vouches for the accuracy of these facts.

THE EXTENT OF INSPIRATION

While the fact of inspiration is recognized by most churches, all do not agree on the extent of inspiration. There are various theories of inspiration.

NATURAL INSPIRATION

This theory identifies inspiration with a high order of human ability. It denies anything supernatural in the preparation of the Scriptures. It claims that the biblical writers were no more inspired than Milton, Shakespeare, or Mohammed.

However, when David said, "The Spirit of the Lord spake by

me, and his word was in my tongue" (II Sam. 23:2), he meant something more than human skill. When Isaiah announced, "Thus saith the Lord" (Isa. 43:1), he claimed something higher than a great poet's eloquence. When Paul said to the Corinthians, "Which things also we speak, not in the words which man's wisdom teacheth, but which the Holy Ghost teacheth" (I Cor. 2:13), he used language for which no parallel can be found in mere human ability.

When one compares the literature of the great secular authors with that of the Bible, the difference between the two is not one simply of degree, but of kind. The Bible is not only a higher plane of literature; but an environment that is altogether different. If the qualifications of Bible writers were the same as those of great secular writers, there would be nothing to assure the readers that Moses, David, and Paul did not make human errors or teach human views of life. The theory of natural inspiration discredits rather than supports the Word of God.

MECHANICAL INSPIRATION

This view ignores human instrumentality in the preparation of the Scriptures and claims that the writers were like robots, as insensible to what they were doing as are piano keys to a musician's touch. Consider the stern Moses, the poetic David, the lovable John, and the scholarly Paul. Careful study of the Scriptures reveals that God used these writers' individualities to reach all kinds of people.

PARTIAL INSPIRATION

The theory of partial inspiration is held by some with a superficial knowledge of the Bible who accept scientists' theories as facts. In the face of apparent discrepancies between scientific theories and Scripture, they conclude that the Bible *contains* the Word of God but that much of it is *not* the Word of God, and therefore need not be accurate. They can thus accept the theory of evolution and reject as not inspired those portions of Scripture which refute it. If Jonah's experiences seem incompatible with scientific findings, or statements about the total depravity of human nature and the eternal punishment of the wicked are unacceptable, this theory of partial inspiration provides a convenient escape. But who is to decide what is and what is not inspired? The theory of partial inspiration leaves people in great uncertainty.

PLENARY INSPIRATION

This is the belief of the Christian church. Plenary, or complete, inspiration is the opposite of partial inspiration. It claims all Scripture to be equally inspired, basing its claim upon II Timothy 3:16, "All scripture is given by inspiration of God."

Much has been said and written in answer to the question, "Does inspiration include the very words of the Bible?" Were the words dictated by the Spirit, or were the writers left to choose their own words? If the entire content of the Bible is completely accurate, it can be seen at once that the words as well as the thoughts must be inspired. Some statements of Scripture are the identical words written or spoken by God himself. The Ten Commandments were written with the "finger of God" (Exod.31:18; 32:16). The handwriting on the wall of Belshazzar's palace was written with "the fingers of a man's hand" (Dan. 5:5). In the New Testament, the voice that was heard at the baptism and the transfiguration of the Lord spoke words that could not be mistaken.

Apart from the exact words, there could be no precision, particularly such precision as is demanded in the Scriptures. The declaration of the writers who were chosen of God to record the Scriptures co ~   for words rather than me

The re

THE NATU

Carefu   od transmitted his Word

DIVINE

In botl   words of God were rep   . 28:19; Dan. 5:5). The   ing permitted to hear (d ever people hear the v   e fire, as thou hast hear   . These divine utterances were later recorded on tables of stone "by the finger of God" (Exod. 31:18; Deut. 9:10) and carried in the ark of the covenant. In the New Testament God honored his Son by speaking from heaven at his baptism (Matt. 3:17), his transfiguration (Matt. 17:5), and before his crucifixion (John 12:28). These divine utterances were carefully and correctly recorded by human writers.

DIVINE DICTATION

God put into the mouths of certain men the very words they should speak and write (Exod. 4:10-15; 34:27; Isa. 8:1, 11, 12; Jer. 1:7; 7:27; 13:12; 30:1, 2; Ezek. 3:10, 11; 24:2; Hab. 2:2). Peter says that when the prophets wrote of Christ they actually had to study the predictions which they themselves wrote, and even then did not fully understand them (I Pet. 1:10-12).

Even more significantly Daniel speaks of God's dictation to him, "I heard, but I understood not." In reply to inquiry for further explanation, God directed, "Go thy way, Daniel; for the words are closed up and sealed till the time of the end" (Dan. 12:9). Daniel was given power to record with infallible accuracy what he heard, although he did not understand it. Yet Daniel was the wise man who interpreted Nebuchadnezzar's dream and deciphered the handwriting upon the wall. His recording of God's dictation without understanding it is no inspiration of mere ideas, nor elevation of mind, nor increase of intellectual power. It is a direct and special revelation of truth from God.

HUMAN EXPRESSION

A Scripture writer's individuality and literary style in relating divine truth was not destroyed by divine inspiration. For instance, the four gospel narrators differed in recording what Pilate wrote upon the cross, yet, by a careful comparison of their accounts (Matt. 27:37; Mark 15:26; Luke 23:38; John 19:19, 20), the exact wording, and what part of it God wished recorded can be determined. The complete inscription evidently was, "This is Jesus of Nazareth, the King of the Jews," but the all-important fact recorded by all four writers was that Jesus was "the King of the Jews." This was the statement which displeased the Jews, for they asked Pilate not to write it. The fact was the Jews quoted accurately these words which applied to the argument and omitted the rest. That is just what the gospel writers did under the guidance of the Holy Spirit. The Holy Spirit employed the attention, investigation, memory, personality, logic—in fact, all the faculties of all the writers—and worked through them.

THE CLAIMS FOR INSPIRATION

The writers themselves claimed to write the Scriptures under the direct influence of the Holy Spirit.

OLD TESTAMENT WRITERS

One cannot read the Old Testament without being impressed with the repetition of such phrases as "Thus saith the Lord," which occurs 1900 times. While this occurs mostly in the prophets, even in the historical books, God is shown in close touch with his people.

It is claimed that such expressions as "the Lord said," "the Lord spoke," "the word of the Lord came," are found 3,808 times in the Old Testament. These writers claiming to have had revelations of the will of God, almost always began their messages with the words, "Thus saith the Lord." Their claims are confirmed by the minuteness and detail of names, times, and places which characterize their messages, and the literal fulfillment of their predictions.

When Moses explained creation, he did not make a single reference to the theories of the origin of the universe believed in ancient Egypt or Babylon with which no doubt he was familiar. This can only be understood by the fact that he was controlled by the Holy Spirit. In the brief chapter on creation (Gen. 1), he claims to transcribe the words of God no less than 14 times. Elsewhere it is written again and again, "The Lord spake unto Moses," "The Lord commanded Moses."

In the historical books the Lord speaks to Joshua, Gideon, Samuel, David, Elijah, Elisha, Ezra, Nehemiah, and many others. The New Testament writers not only confirmed statements in the Old Testament, but expressly stated that they were God's utterances (Matt. 1:22, 23; 2:15; Mark 12:36; Luke 1:70; Acts 1:16).

NEW TESTAMENT WRITERS

The New Testament contains more than 280 quotations from 30 of the 39 Old Testament books, spread over 18 of its 27 books (Matt. 10:20; Mark 13:14). Paul, a scholarly Jew and a member of the Sanhedrin, in becoming a Christian, did not modify his absolute confidence in the inspiration of the Old Testament. It always remained the Holy Scriptures with the same divine authority in establishing Christian truth as his own writings which he knew were inspired (I Cor. 2:13; 14:37; I Thess. 2:13). Paul quotes Scripture from Luke in the same breath as from Deuteronomy (I Tim. 5:18; cf. Deut. 25:4; Luke 10:7). Peter classes Paul's writings with "the other scriptures" (II Pet. 3:1, 2, 16). The discourses of Peter, Stephen, and Paul in the Acts are composed almost entirely of Old Testament quotations.

It is evident from this and many other passages that the writers of the New Testament were conscious that those who were instrumental in producing the Old Testament, as well as themselves, received revelations from God and considered themselves inspired of God to complete the Scriptures. They felt while writing that they were giving expression to the infallible truth of God through the operation of the Holy Spirit. This explains the absence of contradiction which would be natural, especially where writers were so far removed from each other in point of time and circumstance.

JESUS CHRIST

To "bear witness to the truth" was one object of Christ's coming into the world (John 18:37). Nor did he speak from himself, but his Father who sent him and gave him a commandment regarding what he should say and what he should speak (John 12:49). In his farewell prayer Christ said, "I have given unto them the words which thou gavest me" (John 17:6, 8). The following sections explain Christ's attitude toward the Scriptures.

He Regarded Them as Authentic in Their Entirety

He showed this by quoting from the Pentateuch, Prophets, and Psalms (Luke 24:27).

He Applied the Whole Scripture to Himself

He used Isaiah 61:1 in the synagogue at Nazareth (Luke 4:16-21). He also reproached the Jews because, though they searched the Scriptures, they did not find him, for, said he, "they are they which testify of me" (John 5:39).

He Quoted From All the Scriptures as of Equal Authority

One word of the Bible, to Christ, and to his opponents also, was sufficient to end any disagreement. His quotations from Deuteronomy silenced Satan (Matt. 4:4, 7, 10). "What is written in the law?" he asked his critics. With that clear, no further arguments were needed. When some complained about the children singing his praises (Matt. 21:16), he merely replied, "Have ye never read, Out of the mouth of babes and sucklings thou hast perfected praise?" (cf. Ps. 8:2).

He Upheld the Verbal Inspiration of the Scriptures

The Lord maintained strongly the verbal inspiration of the Scriptures: "Till heaven and earth pass, one jot or one tittle shall in no wise pass from the law, till all be fulfilled" (Matt. 5:18). The jot was the smallest Hebrew letter, while the tittle was a little projection distinguishing some letters. Not merely the words, but, according to the Lord, the very letters of the Bible were inspired.

He Accepted the Miracles of the Bible

Christ spoke of the flood and the destruction of Sodom and Gomorrah (Luke 17:26-32) as people today might speak of the feats of the astronauts as unquestioned facts. He alluded to the miraculous death of Lot's wife as a well-known catastrophe. He accepted Jonah's marvelous experiences (Matt. 12:40), as well as the book of Daniel with its miraculous happenings (Matt. 24:15).

SUMMARY

The doctrine of the inspiration of the Bible is of tremendous importance for all Christian doctrines are developed from the Bible and rest upon it for authority. The term *inspiration* is defined as, "God's power enabling man to accurately record the truth revealed."

Several theories of inspiration have been advocated.

The theory of *natural inspiration* identifies inspiration with a high order of human ability. Proponents of this view say that Bible writers were no more inspired than were secular writers. Holding this view discredits the Word of God.

Another view is *mechanical inspiration*. This view ignores human instrumentality in the preparation of the Scriptures and claims that the writers were like robots whom God used to write what he dictated. This view does not recognize the varied styles found in the Bible.

A third view is *partial inspiration* which concludes that the Bible contains God's Word but that much of it is not God's Word, especially when it disagrees with current ideas of scientists. The obvious problem is, who determines what is and what is not inspired? This view leaves one with great uncertainty.

The fourth view is that held by the Christian church—*plenary inspiration*. Using II Timothy 3:16 this view claims that all Scripture is inspired by God. God so directed the biblical writers that even the words they used were inspired and accurate making the entire record inerrant.

When God transmitted his Word to the biblical writers he used several methods. Some parts of the Bible were given as *divine utterances.* These sections are the exact reproductions of God's spoken words. Other sections are *divine dictation.* In these sections God put the very words into the Bible writers' mouths. A third method of recording the Bible could be termed *human expression.* This means that inspiration did not destroy the Scripture writers' individualities and literary styles. This accounts for the differences found in the gospels. The Holy Spirit employed all the faculties of the biblical writers and worked through them.

The writers of both the Old and New Testaments claimed to be writing under direct guidance of the Holy Spirit. Jesus Christ also affirmed the inspiration of the Scriptures and even expressed that the object of his coming was to "bear witness of the truth."

Christ's attitude toward the Scriptures is shown by the fact that: he regarded them as entirely authentic; he applied them to himself; he quoted from all as of equal authority; he upheld their verbal inspiration; and he accepted the miracles recorded in the Bible.

DISCUSSION QUESTIONS

1. Why is the authority of the Bible so essential?
2. Define and compare the terms: revelation, inspiration, and illumination.
3. Define and refute the theories of natural inspiration, mechanical inspiration, and partial inspiration.
4. What is meant by plenary inspiration?
5. Why cannot inspiration be limited to the "thoughts" or "concepts" of the Scriptures?
6. Name or give examples of three important characteristics that express the nature of inspiration.
7. What are some of the claims for inspiration by Old and New Testament writers and the testimony of Christ?
8. How would you justify belief in inspiration of the Bible to one who denies it?

RESOURCES

Hannah, John (ed). *Inerrancy and the Church.* Chicago: Moody Press, 1984.

Pache, Rene. *The Inspiration and Authority of Scripture.* Chicago: Moody Press, 1979.

Saucy, Robert L. *Is the Bible Reliable?* Wheaton, IL: Victor Books, 1983.

Creation and Fall of Man

THE CREATION OF MAN

While Bible scholars differ in their interpretations of how and when God created the world, the Scriptures clearly affirm that God did create the world and placed man in it.

MAN'S ORIGIN

The Bible says that God created man out of dust and gave him life (Gen. 2: 7). This creative act took place completely separate from his creation of the animals. Man is infinitely more than a higher order of the animal kingdom. The biblical account of the divine touch contradicts the possibility of an animal origin or of man's evolving from a lower order of creation.

A Direct Creative Act

Not only in Genesis (5:2), but elsewhere in Scripture (Deut. 4:32; Ps. 100:3) it is taught that the human race originated by a separate creative act of God. This teaching separates man, even in his lowest condition, from the next lower order of creation. Evolution has no explanation for man's higher spiritual nature. The fact of man's supremacy over all other creatures would scarcely have been possible had he been merely one of them.

A Son Of God

Bible genealogies trace the human race back to Adam, but are careful to note that the first man, like the angels, was a son of God[1] (Luke 3:38). The Greeks were too proud and intelligent to claim an animal origin. When Paul quoted the Greek poet (Acts 17:28), he established common ground for Greek history and biblical fact, and demonstrated that the two corresponded.

MAN'S CHARACTER

Man was made last of all the creatures. He could take no honor to himself as contributing toward the work of creation. And as the last of God's creative work he was honored and appointed ruler of the entire creation.

His Material Nature

Man was made of the dust of the ground (Gen. 2:7a), an unlikely material for making a man. His body was formed from materials which the earth supplies. The Bible states what modern chemistry confirms, that all the elements of our physical structure are found in soil which covers the earth (Job 33:6). At its dissolution in death the body returns to its origin—"for dust thou art, and unto dust shalt thou return" (Gen 3:19b); but the spirit returns to its origin—"to God who gave it" (Eccles. 12:7).

His Spiritual Nature

The body was created, and then into it God breathed the breath of life (Gen. 2:7b; Job 33:4). This process was not followed with the members of the animal kingdom, but only with man. God put the breath of heaven into dust of the earth. The spirit dwells in the house of clay and is the life and support of it. The body would be worthless and useless without the spirit to enliven it. At death, the body is committed to the grave, but into God's hands the spirit is committed, for it is from God's hands that it is received.

God's Image In Man

Genesis 1:27 says that God created man in his own image. Man was not made in the likeness of any creature that went before him, but in the likeness of his creator. Yet between God and man there is an infinite distance. Christ alone is the image of God's person, having the same nature (John 14:9; Heb. 1:3). How then is man like God?

[1]According to Scripture usage, the term *son of God* when applied to creatures refers to a being brought into existence by a direct creative act of God. Thus, Adam, angels, and believers are so described. Man after the fall is never called this except when regenerated.

Personality—The divine breath gave man a soul as well as a spirit (I Thess. 5:23; Heb. 4:12). Through his senses man has world-consciousness and through his spirit, God-consciousness. But it is through his soul that he possesses self-consciousness or personality. Personality consists of intellect, emotion, and will. Adam was not a primitive being, slowly groping toward articulate speech, but an intelligent, thinking individual able to provide a suitable name for every creature (Gen. 2:19). He also had the freedom to exercise the power of his will in moral and spiritual choices. Man could not lose this resemblance to his creator and still be a man.

Morality—Man was created pure and upright. His nature conformed to the ideals of right human conduct. However, this phase of his resemblance to his creator was forfeitable, and indeed man did lose it. Adam was created with tendencies *toward* God; since Adam's fall, people are born with tendencies *away from* God. When a person becomes "a new creature in Christ," he is morally reinstated. He is invited to "put off the old man with his deeds;" and to "put on the new man, which is renewed in knowledge after the image of him that created him" (Col. 3:9, 10).

MAN'S HELPMATE

In the beginning, Adam was alone, belonging neither to the upper world of angels nor the lower world of animals. God acknowledged this fact when he said, "It is not good that man should be alone" (Gen. 2:18a). Therefore God graciously provided companionship for him.

Woman, as man, was created by a special act of God (Gen. 2:21, 22; I Tim. 2:13). However, she was not made of dust, but of man. Man was dust refined, but woman was dust twice refined, one step further from the earth. While Eve was created, Adam slept, not only that the operation might be painless, but that God alone might be author of the new creature.

Genesis describes the true relationship between man and woman (2:23, 24). One is but the complement of the other. The two together make a perfect unity (Matt. 19:4-6). Matthew Henry says: "The woman was formed out of man, not out of his head to rule over him, not out of his feet to be a doormat, but out of his side to be his equal."

MAN'S DOMINION

Man is God's deputy or representative. He is ruler over the natural creation. His maker assigned him this place of preeminence (Gen. 1:26-30; 2:19, 20; Ps. 8:3-8).

His Authority

Many evidences provide a living witness to man's authority over nature. The constant advances of science characterizing our space age, such as orbital travel, global communication, and other technological developments, reflect the God-ordained power of man to harness the mysterious forces of nature.

His Responsibility

In accepting authority over the Garden of Eden, Adam was given a responsibility. He was commanded "to dress it and to keep it" (Gen. 2:15-17). If the Hebrew word is here translated "preserve," as it is in a later chapter, it would suggest the possibility of someone contesting Adam's right to ownership. This makes it easier to understand why Satan should try to gain control over Adam and Eve. When he found this inferior creature, Adam, over the kingdom which he once governed, Satan was aroused to intense jealousy and hatred and sought any means to defeat God and seize man's inheritance from him.

THE FALL OF MAN

In the story of Job we are admitted to the councils of heaven, and we hear God giving Satan permission to test Job. Perhaps a similar scene had been enacted before the fall of Adam, at which time Satan intimated that Adam could not resist evil. He might have argued that a weakling who would fall before temptation would not be a fit subject to take an angel's place as ruler over the earth. As God later allowed Satan to try Job, He also must have allowed him to test Adam.

THE TEMPTATION

Satan laid his plans carefully. He attacked Eve in Adam's absence, knowing that one would yield more easily than two. It is probable that he tempted her near the tree. She had time for reflection and thought. He was careful to conceal his true character as God's enemy. He did not begin by telling of his own fall, or by speaking boastfully of his own rebellion. He pretended to be friendly toward Eve.

Doubting God's Goodness

Satan spoke politely of God the creator, yet by a sly question he suggested unkindness in the form of an unnecessary and unreasonable restriction. He acted as if it were difficult to believe God could have treated them so unkindly. He planted a doubt in Eve's mind as to the fairness of God's dealing. This is evident from her reply. Although she gave Satan a full account of the law God had laid down, she made certain changes in her statement, indicating she already suspected there was some truth in Satan's inquiry. God had said, "Of every tree of the garden thou mayest freely eat" (Gen. 2:16, 17), but in restating the divine command (3:1-3), Eve left out the word "freely," thereby implying God's strictness instead of his generosity.

She also added the words "neither shall ye touch it." God had not required this but she subtracted from God's permission and added to his prohibition.

In the third place, she downplayed the penalty for disobedience. God had said, "In the day that thou eatest thereof thou shalt surely die," but Eve softened this to "lest ye die."

Denying God's Truthfulness

Satan, greatly encouraged by Eve's reply, saw she was already wavering, and boldly declared that Adam and Eve would not surely die (Gen. 3:4). Then Eve gave a ready ear to Satan's lie.

The devil could do little then, and he can do little now, except as openings are made for him by those he tempts. It was Eve's initial unbelief, shown by her "lest ye die" which encouraged Satan's attack. He intimated that although God was not good enough to let Adam and Eve have full liberty in the garden, He was too good to put them to death for disobedience.

Discovering God's Secrets

Satan appealed to Eve's curiosity and pride by insinuating that God was hiding something from her. He even led her to believe that God had made the prohibition for fear those human creatures might become his equal (Gen. 3:5). Satan had ruined himself by desiring to be like God (Isa. 14:14), and he sought to ruin Adam and Eve by infecting them with the same desire.

THE TRANSGRESSION

Unresisted Impression Of Sin

Satan used three avenues of approach and met with no opposition. Eve's first steps toward willful disobedience were in listening, looking, and lusting.

Eve lost ground just as soon as she began to argue with Satan (Gen. 3:2,3). If she had remembered God's goodness, she would have replied differently.

Satan next opened Eve's impressionable eyes to the forbidden fruit (Gen. 3:6a). Through the eye either fires of devotion or sparks of temptation are kindled.

The final appeal was to the heart. Eve had heard and seen, and now she coveted the enticing fruit which had been expressly forbidden (Gen. 3:6b). Had she been wholehearted in her love for God, she would have rejected the thought of displeasing him. But Satan had already shaken her confidence in God's love.

Unrestrained Expression Of Sin

To covet may be at first an inward sin only, but, unless resisted, it leads to outward expression. Here are three downward steps (Gen. 3:6c): touching, tasting, tempting.

After telling Satan God had commanded that the tree should not even be touched, she came to believe that she would not surely die even if she picked this enticing fruit.

It was not enough to take the forbidden fruit into her hands; she must eat it if she were to realize Satan's promise of advance in knowledge. She felt she must have wisdom, and she must have it at all risks and without delay.

Eve no sooner fell than she became a tempter. Instead of consulting Adam before she took the fatal step, or warning him after she had fallen, she enticed him to share her sin. But there was an hour of reckoning for the guilty pair.

THE TRIBUNAL

The Prosecution

The disobedient subjects were then arraigned before the righteous judge of heaven and earth (Gen. 3:9-11). To God's question, "Where art thou?" the trembling Adam did not confess his guilt, but revealed it by his very fear and shame. Adam was afraid to appear before God because he was naked. Of the obviously guilty pair the judge asked, "Who told thee that thou wast naked? Hast thou eaten of the tree, whereof I commanded thee that thou shouldest not eat?"

The Plea

The guilty pair had an opportunity to answer why they should not be punished for their sin. But instead of confessing guilt, Adam blamed Eve and she blamed the serpent (Gen. 3:12, 13).

He had not a word to say for himself. Adam blamed not only Eve, but God for his trouble. "The woman whom thou gavest to be with me, she gave me of the tree, and I did eat." God made no answer to this foolish excuse but turned to the woman, "What is this that thou hast done?"

The woman likewise refused to make an honest confession of guilt. "The serpent beguiled (deceived) me, and I did eat," was her answer. Admitting the subtlety and deceitfulness of Satan did not justify her in God's sight. Her excuse was no better than her husband's.

The Punishments

The judge proceeded to pass sentence (Gen. 3:14-19).

Degradation fell upon the serpent itself. No other animal shows so sharp a contrast between its keen intellectual powers and its creeping, squirming degradation. The final doom was also pronounced upon Satan, the instigator of the serpent's actions. Christ, the seed of the woman, would some day crush his head.

God predicted suffering and subordination for the woman. Pregnancy and childbirth would be painful. The woman would also be subordinate to her husband.

Physical hardships, painful toil, disappointing problems, and hard struggles were appointed as man's lot, who was also judged a guilty sinner. Formerly the soil had yielded its produce easily and freely in great abundance. Now the man would struggle to make it produce life's necessities.

Thorns and thistles would multiply until they became a burden to man and beast. Job 31:38-40 and Isaiah 7:23, 24 refer to them as judgments, and our Lord spoke of them as injurious (Matt. 13:7).

In addition, Adam's sin caused sin to enter the human race, making all mankind guilty of sin.

SUMMARY

Only God knows exactly how and when the world was created. But he did create it and placed man in it. Man came into being by God's direct creative act making man a high order of creation above the animal kingdom.

Man's character has a three-fold nature—body, spirit, and soul. God formed man's body from dust. Man's spirit and soul came into being when God breathed into him the breath of life. The soul expresses itself in man's personality and morality.

Having no one with whom to share his life caused Adam to become lonely. God acknowledged this and provided woman to be his companion. Woman was also created by God. She was created from man while he slept, making God alone the creator.

As God's representative, man was to rule over the animals and keep the garden where he lived.

But Satan contested man's right of ownership. Satan, taking the form of a serpent, tempted the woman. Satan caused the woman to doubt God's goodness, to deny God's truthfulness, and to try to discover the secrets of God. As a result the woman succumbed to the temptation and ate from the forbidden tree of the knowledge of good and evil. Then Adam did likewise.

God dealt out punishment on all the parties to this first sin. The serpent was cursed and made to crawl on his belly. Later, when Christ came, he would crush Satan's head. The woman was to bear pain in childbirth and be subordinate to the man. The man would have to toil long hours to gain life's necessities.

DISCUSSION QUESTIONS

1. React to the theory of evolution from your study of the Genesis account of creation.
2. What three characteristics can be observed in man's creation?
3. Why did Satan become jealous of man?
4. How does the setting of the first chapter of Job suggest a similar scene before the fall of Adam?
5. In what ways did Satan cast a doubt on God's goodness?
6. How did Satan appeal to Eve's curiosity?
7. Describe the first three steps in Eve's willful disobedience.
8. Describe the three steps that completed her unrestrained expression to sin.
9. What excuse did Adam and Eve make for their sin?
10. Discuss the extent of the consequences of Adam's disobedience.

RESOURCES

Flynn, Leslie B. *What Is Man?* Wheaton, IL: Victor Books, 1983.

Youngblood, Ronald. *How It All Began.* Ventura, CA: Regal Books, 1980.

Faith and Regeneration

FAITH

The King James Version defines faith in Hebrews 11:1 as "the *substance* of things hoped for, the *evidence* of things not seen." The New American Standard Version says in the same verse, "Now faith is the *assurance* of things hoped for, the *conviction* of things not seen."

Faith is belief based on facts. The gospel is a statement of definite, historical facts which the Old Testament saints were confident would occur and which the New Testament saints believed had occurred. "I declare unto you the gospel which I preached unto you," said Paul; and then he made plain exactly what the gospel is: "How that Christ died for our sins according to the scriptures; and that he was buried, and that he rose again the third day according to the scriptures" (I Cor. 15:1-4). Here are three tremendous facts: the substitutionary death of Christ; his burial; and his resurrection.

But faith is more than a recognition of facts. A person may know all about Christ as revealed in the Bible, may even believe God's Word to be true, and yet not have real faith in Christ as his personal Savior. Agreement by the mind is not the same as surrender of the heart. Satan and the fallen angels believe in God to the extent that they tremble for fear of him (James 2:19). Faith not only accepts but also believes and applies the facts. Faith involves the affections and the will, as well as the intellect. Faith harmonizes the will and the understanding.

Faith is "the conviction of things not seen." Faith enables the seeking soul to penetrate into the spiritual realm. Faith is the source of all spiritual achievement. "By it the men of old gained approval" (Heb. 11:2, NAS). Abel, Enoch, Noah, Abraham, Isaac, Jacob, and many others have their names inscribed in the Bible's hall of fame, not because of their wealth or wisdom or worldly achievements, but because of their faith. Faith is the supreme requirement for heaven's favor. "Without faith it is impossible to please him: for he that cometh to God must believe that he is, and that he is a rewarder of them that diligently seek him" (Heb. 11:6).

SAVING FAITH

Adam's sin brought death to the human race. "Dust thou art, and unto dust shalt thou return" (Gen. 3:19) was the divine decree issued to the first parents. The all-important question that every person must ask is, "If a man die, shall he live again?" (Job 14:14). People may want one thing today and another tomorrow, but at the time of death the one thing they want above everything else is life, which can be had only through Christ. "I am come that they might have life" (John 10:10).

Saving faith produces salvation from the penalty of sin (John 3:16-18), and belief in the only Savior appointed for this purpose. Without faith in Christ, a person will be deprived of heaven's happiness through eternity (John 3:36). He must share forever the punishment that has been prepared for the devil and his angels (Matt. 25:41).

Those with saving faith believe with the heart (Acts 16:31), and confess with the mouth (Matt. 10:32). With the heart there is recognition that the Lord Jesus is the sinner's substitute, and with the mouth there is confession not only of a hopeless condition, but of the Lord Jesus Christ as personal Savior (Rom. 10:8-11).

Upon Calvary's three crosses hung three representatives of the human race (Luke 23:39-43). The two malefactors were alike in their sin. They were alike in their condemnation. But in their last moments one cruelly mocked the Lord and called him an imposter, unable to save himself and these guilty thieves, while the other rebuked his companion's blasphemy and then took the necessary steps for salvation. He recognized the justice and judgment of

God, admitted his own guilt, confessed the Savior, and asked for salvation. Here was a man who in his dying breath had faith enough to recognize Jesus as king. No wonder the Lord said to him, "Today shalt thou be with me in paradise" (Luke 23:43).

LIVING FAITH

Faith is required not only for preservation from the *penalty* of sin but also for deliverance from the *power* of sin. When people once understand the love of God as expressed in Jesus Christ, they are not to continue in sin. How then are they to persevere when they are tempted?

God uses temptation to test faith. Not that God tempts people, for God is not the author of evil (James 1:13,14), but he allows Satan to do so. God *tests*, but Satan *tempts*. Moreover, Satan's temptations can be recognized, for they are common to all people and they can be resisted, for a way of escape has been promised (I Cor. 10:13). Believers are to rejoice in the midst of temptation since it is proof of God's loving discipline (James 1:2,3).

The only one who can deliver us from temptation is the Lord Jesus Christ (Heb. 2:18; II Pet. 2:9), who is the author and finisher of our faith (Heb. 12:2). He was tempted in all points as we are and yet was without sin. Faith in his victory and his power is the shield with which we are "able to quench all the fiery darts of the wicked one" (Eph. 6:16).

WORKING FAITH

Sinners are saved by faith, not by works, but it is by works that they demonstrate and prove their faith. Christians are God's "workmanship, created in Christ Jesus unto good works, which God hath before ordained that we should walk in them" (Eph. 2:10). Though not created in Christ Jesus *by* good works, believers are created *unto* or *for* good works (Tit. 2:14). Works do not justify people, but justified people work.

Work is the fruit of faith. An inactive Christian life is empty and unfruitful. Work is not the foundation but the completion of faith. James is called the apostle of works, but he does not minimize the importance of faith (2:14-26). True faith will express itself in actions. James teaches that where there are no good works there is not true religion, and a faith that is not producing good works is of no value. Actions must be regarded as the evidence of a justified person.

REGENERATION

Saving faith and regeneration are inseparable. The moment people believe in Christ, they are born of God. The weakness of their faith may make them unaware of the change, just as newborn infants know little or nothing about themselves. But where there is saving faith, there is always new birth, and where there is no faith there is no regeneration.

NECESSITY OF THE NEW BIRTH

Mankind's Depravity

The fall of Adam becomes tremendously more important when we discover it was our fall, for the entire human race has inherited Adam's sinful nature (Jer. 17:9). As David, the man after God's own heart, confessed, "I was shapen in iniquity" (Ps. 51:5). Paul put it even stronger when he said that "the carnal mind is enmity against God" (Rom. 8:7). It is not only corrupt, but corruption. It is not only wicked, but wickedness itself (Rom. 7:18).

God's Holiness

When Adam and Eve lost their original righteousness, they at once forfeited communion with their creator (Hab. 1:13). No one has ever been admitted to heaven in his sins. No one can see God without a pure heart (Matt. 5:8). No one can come into his sacred presence unless he is partaker of the divine nature (II Pet. 1:4). God's holiness requires holiness in his children.

It is only when people begin to understand something of the unchangeably holy nature of God that they come to realize how absolutely unfitted they are in their natural condition to have fellowship with him.

Certainty of Death

Everyone must die (Rom. 5:12; 7:5). As the Scriptures point out, one of the direct consequences of sin is universal death. Between Genesis 1 which records the creation of Adam and Genesis 3 which records his death, stands the fall of man and the entrance of sin.

There is nothing that people can do to overcome death. In spite of their scientific advances, they still die.

God, however, has made provision for this human predicament. The whole story is presented simply and wonderfully in the familiar verse, John 3:16. Everlasting life is given to those who accept the offer of God's love shown in Jesus Christ. The presentation in Romans 5 notes that while Adam brought death upon the human race, Jesus Christ brought life. Another familiar reference, Romans 6:23, pictures clearly this contrast between death and life.

NATURE OF THE NEW BIRTH

Exactly when the new birth takes place cannot be told any more than the exact moment that darkness blends into dawn can be demonstrated. Just how the new birth takes place is impossible to explain (John 3:7,8), but the Bible says it is as instantaneous as all of God's works of creation. "He spake, and it was done." But although it is not known when and how, it is sure that the new birth has taken place by the evidences that accompany this miracle.

It is possible for people to improve their condition to such an extent that they may be deceived into believing they have experienced regeneration. Thousands of good people have never been born again and are still "dead in trespasses and sins." It is well, therefore, to know the nature of regeneration.

More Than Natural Descent

The Jews were God's chosen people, but to be born of Hebrew parents was no guarantee of salvation. Esau was a child of the covenant but he sold his birthright for a single meal (Heb. 12:16, 17). Nadab and Abihu were the sons of the high priest but they were so godless that they were destroyed by fire (Lev. 10:1,2).

The blessing of being born into a godly Christian family does not automatically grant salvation. Regeneration is not the result of human birth or earthly relationship.

More Than Human Decision

The new birth is not self-reformation, though many would like to think so. Education and enlightenment will not make sinners holy. The meanest kind of scoundrel is an educated scoundrel, and the most detestable criminal is the enlightened hypocrite. Joash was well educated by Jehoiada, the high priest, but as soon as his faithful instructor died, he fell into evil ways (II Chron. 24:2, 17, 18). Saul of Tarsus was also well educated but that did not keep him from persecuting the church (Phil. 3:4-6).

More Than Human Determination

As much as Christian parents desire and urge their children to experience the new birth, regeneration comes only from God. Christian parents who know the Lord and desire their children to have the same experience should not pressure their offspring into making an early decision. Far better it is to obey God's command to "bring up children in the nurture and admonition of the Lord" and to take the Lord at his word in Proverbs 22:6, "Train up a child in the way he should go: and when he is old he will not depart from it." Exposure to Christianity as living and working faith, constant prayer, and trust in God must take the place of human determination.

Being Born of God

Regeneration starts with God and ends with God. The faith that justifies is the work of God, by which the old nature is crucified and believers are made into the likeness of Christ (Eph. 2:1,4,5), thus becoming new creatures and children of God. The new birth is a new creation. Believers are born from above, not of corruptible seed, but of incorruptible. The new birth is the supernatural work of the Holy Spirit (John 3:5).

NOBILITY OF THE NEW BIRTH

Adam was not a child born of natural descent, nor of human decision or determination, but of God. A restored or regenerated son is as marvelous a creation as Adam. There is nothing higher than being admitted to sonship with God.

Partakers of Divine Nature (II Pet. 1:4)

Unregenerated people are intellectually blind to spiritual privileges and corrupt in their affections. In the new birth, God imparts his own wise and holy nature, a nature that thinks as God thinks, feels as God feels, wills as God wills.

Human Bodies Become Temples of the Holy Spirit (I Cor. 6:19)

It is almost unbelievable that the Holy Spirit condescends to dwell with people. And yet we know that our Lord's parting gift to his disciples was the abiding presence of the third person of the Trinity. Since Pentecost he has not only been the governor and director of the church, but the personal companion of each individual member.

Regenerated People Can Overcome The World (I John 5:4)

Real Christians on their way to heaven have a challenge to fulfill. They must overcome the world because the world is under Satan's dominion. As its prince and ruler, he finds temptations suited to everyone. The smile of the world and hope of its favor make many traitors to God. The fear of its frown keeps many from confessing Christ. But Christians lose their love for the world and the things of the world, and confess that they are pilgrims and strangers on this earth, looking for a city whose builder and maker is God.

Regenerated People Become Sin Conquerors (I John 3:9)

Being born again does not mean that people have already attained perfection. Sin is still present, but it no longer has power. The new nature imparted in regeneration makes the continuous practice of sin impossible. To live in sin is contrary to the new nature of which they have been made partakers. As the whole nature of God hates sin, so those who are partakers of the divine nature come likewise to turn from and hate evil.

Regenerated People Love Others (I John 3:14; 4:7)

Love is the atmosphere of heaven. God never said, "Thou shalt not" to the angels because they always love him with all their being. People who have experienced the second birth love their enemies as well as their friends and thus prove that they are partakers of the divine nature. "See how those Christians love" was the comment of observers on the character of the early church members.

SUMMARY

Faith and regeneration are God's way for mankind to overcome the sinful nature which they inherit from Adam.

Faith is belief based on facts. There are three types of faith—saving, living, and working.

Saving faith is the recognition of salvation from the penalty of sin. In order for people to acquire saving faith they must first recognize the justice and judgment of God. Second, they must admit their guilt. And third, they must confess the Savior before others.

Faith is needed not only to save from death, but also to live the Christian life. *Living faith* delivers the believer from the power of sin. Satan's temptations test our faith. In times of testing the believer needs to draw closer to God and he will provide the strength needed to stand up to any temptation.

Working faith is the outward manifestation of living faith. Working faith expresses itself not so much in words but in actions. Works do not justify people, but justified people work.

Saving faith and regeneration are inseparable. Where there is faith there is always regeneration.

Regeneration (the new birth) is necessary because it is demanded by mankind's depravity, God's holiness, and the certainty of death.

John 1:13 explains the nature of the new birth. It is more than natural descent, human decision, or human determination. It is being born of God. Regeneration is the supernatural work of the Holy Spirit.

Regenerated people become partakers of the divine nature, have bodies which are temples of the Holy Spirit, are able to overcome and conquer the powers of sin and the world, and love others.

DISCUSSION QUESTIONS

1. What is the biblical definition of faith?
2. Define saving faith.
3. How is saving faith illustrated in the case of the penitent thief on the cross at Calvary?
4. Give an illustration of living faith.
5. Define working faith.
6. What is the relationship between faith and regeneration?
7. Why is the new birth necessary?
8. What is meant by the depravity of mankind?
9. Using John 1:13 explain the nature of the new birth.
10. How have people tried to save themselves?
11. In what ways is a Christian as marvelous a creation as Adam?
12. What conquests are made possible for regenerated people?
13. How would you explain the new birth to an unsaved person?
14. How can a person experience salvation in Christ?

RESOURCES

Chafer, Lewis S. *Salvation*. Grand Rapids: Zondervan Pub. House, 1972.

Ryrie, Charles C. *A Survey of Bible Doctrine*. Chicago: Moody Press, 1972.

Justification and Adoption

JUSTIFICATION

Justification is a legal term implying a clearing of one's name, the winning of a favorable verdict, whether it be in a court of law, of public opinion, or of conscience. God's justification is not for the righteous, but for the wicked. Hence, justification is the judicial act of God whereby guilty sinners, who put their faith in Jesus Christ as Savior and Lord, are declared righteous in his eyes and freed from guilt and punishment.

PROCESS OF JUSTIFICATION

The process of justification is simple enough to all who understand and appreciate God's grace. But mankind's sinful nature makes it difficult to realize the extent of God's love and mercy, or to accept His unmerited favor.

The process of justification includes the forgiveness of sin, the application of Christ's righteousness, and is conditional upon faith.

Passages in Scripture that declare God's willingness to forgive sin and remove the death penalty include: Ps. 130:4; Mic. 7:18, 19; Acts 13:38, 39; Rom. 8:1, 33, 34; Col. 2:13, 14.

Everyone has sinned. All sin offends God. His whole nature is turned against it. If all the sins of a person's life were recorded, they would make an almost endless list, for "There is none righteous, no, not one" (Rom. 3:10).

It is God who justifies. People cannot justify themselves. Only because of Christ's atoning death on the cross can God cleanse sinners and justify them completely. How marvelous that God who intensely hates sin can so greatly love the sinner. Justification is far more than pardon. Sinners desperately need to be released from their guilt to save them from the judgment of a holy and righteous God. The forgiven sinner receives more benefit than even a discharged criminal. The righteousness of Jesus Christ, God's beloved Son, is credited to his account (Rom. 3:22; 5:17-21).

A good illustration of this principle is found in Paul's letter to Philemon at Colosse concerning Onesimus, Philemon's runaway slave. Onesimus had stolen some of his master's money and fled to Rome where he wasted it. But while Onesimus was able to hide from his master in the great city, he could not get away from God. Under Paul's preaching, he was converted. Repentant of his crime, Onesimus prepared to go back and make amends to his master. He carried with him an important letter to Philemon. Paul wrote of the great change that had taken place in Onesimus and made the following request: "But if he has wronged you in any way, or owes you anything, charge that to my account" (Philemon 18, NAS).

God accepts the believer through Christ and in every case where the believer has wronged God, Christ has sustained the guilt and penalty (I Cor. 1:30). What the believer owes God in complete obedience, but could never pay, Christ has paid for him.

Saving faith is both a condition of regeneration and of justification. Paul uses the life of Abraham as an illustration of justification by faith (Rom. 4). He states that righteousness was applied, counted, imputed to the patriarch without works. Abraham never questioned the promises of God, remote and seemingly impossible as they must have seemed. He was *fully persuaded* that whatever God promised He would do (v. 21). It is this kind of trust in God that the believer must have in order to be justified.

Justification is the free gift of God (I Cor. 6:11). It is *freely* by his grace (Rom. 3:24). God "hath raised us up together, and made us sit together in heavenly places in Christ Jesus: that in the ages to come he might show the exceeding riches of his grace in his kindness toward us through Christ Jesus" (Eph. 2:6, 7).

The only way a righteous and just God could forgive sin was to provide a sinless substitute (Isa. 53:11). To overlook sin would cancel his holiness and bring moral chaos into the world. Only by the death of the perfect Son of God could the penalty be paid for all mankind (Rom. 5:9; II Cor. 5:21). The Old Testament sacrifices foreshadowed the supreme sacrifice to come, for "without shedding of blood is no remission" of sin (Heb. 9:22-28; I John 1:7).

MARVELS OF JUSTIFICATION

God's justification means more than pardon. It provides salvation and security and includes peace, joy, and eternal glory.

The enmity between sinners and God is ended by the cross. The moment sinners believe in Christ they are justified and have peace with God. It is not a mere truce or even an armistice, but a permanent and abiding relationship.

The joy of justification springs from the assured hope of a glorious future and is distinctly the Christian's heritage. In contrast, "no hope" is the characteristic description of those without Christ. Of all people believers should be the most happy and joyful. They are at peace with God and will enjoy him forever.

"In the world ye shall have tribulation" (John 16:33), the Lord told his disciples, and his purpose is understood by those who have been justified. Realizing their sonship changes believers' attitudes toward suffering. The justified know "that the sufferings of this present time are not worthy to be compared with the glory which shall be revealed in us" (Rom. 8:18).

Christ in his farewell prayer asked that the disciples might be with him to be partakers of his glory (John 17:22-24). Nothing can compare with the amazing grace of Jesus the Lord who consented to allow people to share his glory.

ADOPTION

Adoption means the "placing of a son." It is a Roman word, for adoption was little known among the Jews. It means the taking voluntarily of a child of other parents to be one's own child, bestowing on him all the advantages of a child by birth. It is used of the believer when the question of rights, privileges, and inheritance are involved. God's adoption of believers into his own family shows his grace and gives believers a new status. They are not slaves but sons, possessing all the rights of children as well as the inheritance from the Father.

PARTICIPANTS OF ADOPTION
The Nation Israel

"Who are Israelites, to whom pertaineth the adoption," said Paul (Rom. 9:4). Comparing this with Deuteronomy 14:2 and Isaiah 43:1, it is evident that the reference is to Israel's being the chosen people of God. "I have redeemed thee, I have called thee by thy name; thou art mine," the Lord said to Israel.

God's marvelous protecting and delivering power was exercised over Israel. To them his precious promises were given. They were his children by his own choice. But, they chose otherwise. They turned against God as their Father, completing their rejection in refusing the promised Redeemer, the very Son of God.

Believers

The loving heart of God still yearned for a people of his own on whom he might shower the abundance of his grace. Thus God opened the door to the Gentiles. "But as many as received him, to them gave he power to become the sons of God, even to them that believe on his name" (John 1:12). Israel was God's son, but now under the gospel individual believers, either Jews or Gentiles, receive the adoption of sons.

Adoption gives a godly nature (Gal. 4:6)—All who are adopted into the family of God partake of his nature, for he will have all his children to resemble him.

Adoption gives equal rights to all sons (Gal. 4:7)—All God's children are heirs. In some countries, the children do not share their father's estate equally unless he so wills, but the eldest son is the heir. In the family of God all the children are declared joint-heirs with Christ, the first-born (Rom. 8:17).

Adoption gives fellowship (II Cor. 6:17, 18)—Adoption involves the fellowship of Father and child. Adoption is an eternal agreement; only as Christians separate themselves from sin, setting their affections on things above, can they know the fellowship of Father and child.

TIME OF ADOPTION

When does adoption into the family of heaven take place? Adoption is a past, present, and future act.

Eternal In God's Plan

Christ's sacrificial death and the adoption of believers was planned by God ages before they actually happened. Not only did God, before the foundation of the world, choose to have a heavenly family of earth-born mortals, but he knew which individuals would be adopted (Eph. 1:4,5).

Received When One Believes

The actual act of adoption cannot take place for the individual until he is born again; that is, until he believes fully in Jesus Christ for salvation. A holy God cannot receive into his family an unrepentant child. However, adoption takes place the moment one believes in Christ. Sonship is the *present* possession of the believer (Gal. 3:26; I John 3:2).

But how can God's predestination of those to be adopted (Eph. 1:5) be reconciled with man's free will to determine his adoption? (John 1:12). Suppose that over the door of a great building is written, WHOSOEVER WILL, LET HIM COME IN. A person accepts the invitation and enters. But after he is inside he sees on the other side of the door, PREDESTINED TO BE ADOPTED. He is satisfied. He finds no fault with either inscription. An unbeliever cannot understand adoption. His first concern is salvation, but once he accepts God's gracious plan, he learns that he has not only been regenerated and justified, but adopted into the family of God.

Completed At the Lord's Return

The full revelation of a believer's status as a son of God is reserved for a future day (Eph. 1:10,11). Here in this world Christians are not accepted as the sons of the mighty God, but some day they will appear like Jesus Christ (Col. 3:4, I John 3:1,2).

RESULTS OF ADOPTION
No Longer Under Tutors Or Bondage

"But after that faith is come, we are no longer under a schoolmaster" (Gal. 3:25). The Greek word translated *schoolmaster* means a trusted slave who cared for a child until he was twelve. He kept him from physical and moral evil and accompanied him constantly. He gave him commands and prohibitions and limited his freedom. All this was done to train the child for adult responsibilities. Thus the law was meant to lead people to Christ to show them their sin and condemnation, in order that they might recognize their need of a Redeemer. This purpose being accomplished, people are no longer under the law, but are adopted as adult-sons when they are born again.

Israel was placed under the law and thus was in constant bondage and fear through lack of perfect obedience. Jehovah was teaching a sinful people his holiness, and to draw near to him was possible only by sacrifice. But when Christ came, all was different.

But Now "Sons of God"

"And if children, then heirs; heirs of God, and joint-heirs with Christ" (Rom. 8:17). If a man is really a child of God he becomes God's heir. When children inherit their parents' wealth it is because they were born into their parents' family. It is not because they do anything. Their parents bestow the inheritance on them. The young ruler said, "What must I do to inherit?" This is a contradiction in itself! Ages and ages of ever-increasing blessings are promised to believers as joint-heirs.

BLESSINGS OF ADOPTION

A Heavenly Family

Adoption into the family of heaven provides a family name, family likeness, and family love.

How can anyone be like God? It seems impossible for a human creature, but to be like God is to be like Christ, who is "the express image of his person" (Heb. 1:3). Christ is God, expressing himself in language that humans can understand. Christ is the great pattern for heaven's family. To be "imitators of our Lord Jesus Christ" in the true biblical sense is to reveal the characteristics of the heavenly family.

Christians cannot pray "our Father" and then despise their brethren. Family love demands that they live and act as brothers and sisters should. They must, like Christ, love those who differ from them in language and custom, even those who do not yet know their Father (John 13:35; Rom. 5:5; I John 3:14).

A Heavenly Father

Christ taught his followers to pray, "Our Father which art in heaven," in order that they might understand and appropriate God's provision, comfort and correction. Since God is the Christian's Father he hears and answers their prayers and provides for all their needs (Matt. 7:11).

"Like as a father pitieth his children, so the Lord pitieth them that fear him" (Ps. 103:13). With his pity goes his perfect comfort, "I, even I, am he that comforteth you" (Isa. 51:12). At best, an earthly father's consolation can only be temporary. Grief and sorrow cannot be avoided, but "the God of all comfort . . . comforteth us" (II Cor. 1:3,4).

If Christ, God's only Son, suffered that believers might be adopted into the family of heaven, what better treatment could be expected by adopted sons? "The servant is not greater than his Lord." Why should Christians expect that God will nourish his adopted sons with less love and less rigorous discipline than he did his only begotten Son? "As many as I love, I rebuke and chasten," God says (Rev. 3:19; cf. Heb. 12:5-11), and he constantly corrects his beloved children for their own good.

A Heavenly Inheritance

Since Christians are the adopted children of God, heaven is their inheritance. This legacy which the heavenly Father bestows as the proof of his love is incorruptible and undefiled.

The inheritance will not perish as do earthly fortunes. It is an everlasting possession which neither moth nor rust can corrupt nor thieves steal.

The inheritance will lose none of its brilliance and splendor. The crown of glory, though worn for millions of ages, will not be dimmed. The golden streets will lose none of their lustre. God's children will never grow weary of heaven.

SUMMARY

Justification is an act of God whereby guilty sinners, who put their faith in Christ as Savior and Lord, are declared righteous in his eyes and freed from guilt and punishment.

The process of justification unfolds in three steps. The first is the forgiving of sin. Because everyone has sinned, everyone needs God's forgiveness. The second step is the application of Christ's righteousness. Justification is more than pardon. When sinners accept God's forgiveness they discover that the righteousness of Jesus Christ is credited to their account. Finally, the process of justification is conditioned upon faith. When sinners are justified they become fully persuaded that whatsoever God promised, he will do. They accept it as a free gift of God through the shedding of Christ's blood.

When sinners are justified they receive many blessings. Among these are: peace with God, joy, and title to eternal glory. They are adopted into the family of God with full rights and privileges as sons and daughters.

The participants of adoption in the Old Testament were the Israelites. But when they rejected Christ, God opened the way for everyone who believes.

From the beginning God planned this adoption. He planned that it would take place at the time the individual believes in Christ for salvation. However, the full revelation of the status of adoption will not be complete until Christ returns at which time believers will be made like him.

When believers are adopted into God's family they are no longer under the law, but are adopted as sons. They no longer have the bondage of fear for not keeping the law perfectly, but they are now sons of God and joint-heirs with Christ.

When believers are adopted by God, they are part of the heavenly family. They take on God's family name, his family likeness, and share his family love. As children of God Christians are recipients of his fatherly provision, comfort, and correction. And finally, Christians have a heavenly inheritance. As proof of his love, the heavenly Father bestows on his children an incorruptible, undefiled, and unfading inheritance—heaven.

DISCUSSION QUESTIONS

1. What does justification mean as related to the sinner's position before God?
2. Describe the process whereby a sinner is justified.
3. What is meant by the application of Christ's righteousness?
4. How is faith related to justification?
5. What is meant by adoption in relationship to the believer?
6. What benefits are conferred in the adoption of believers?
7. How is adoption related to the past, present, and future?
8. Write your own definitions of justification and adoption.

RESOURCES

Henry, Carl H. F. (ed). *Fundamentals of the Faith.* Grand Rapids: Zondervan Pub. House, 1969. Chapter 9.

Ryrie, Charles C. *A Survey of Bible Doctrine.* Chicago: Moody Press, 1972. Chapter 7.

Worship and Prayer

WORSHIP

An important function of the church is the public worship service. Family members gather together daily for family worship. Many individuals set aside time each day for private worship. What is worship? Reading the Word of God, listening to a sermon, praying, and singing are contributing factors to worship, but they can be done without worshiping.

The root of the word translated "worship" in the Old Testament means "to bow down." However worship is more than a physical act or intellectual exercise. Worship, as used in the Bible, is concentrating on God and thinking about his power and majesty, thus turning attention away from oneself. Worship is a spiritual activity. "God is a Spirit: and they that worship him must worship him in spirit and in truth" (John 4:24).

The need for worship is as natural as the need for protection and love. People worship a variety of things in an attempt to fill this need. But only when the focus of worship is God can this desire be fulfilled.

THE OBJECT OF WORSHIP
God

It is evident from the very first of the Ten Commandments that men will worship other gods (Exod. 20:3). Israel, the highly favored nation to whom God revealed his majesty and his might, was forbidden to substitute other objects of worship (Matt. 4:10). However, despite the solemn warning that any Israelite who worshiped the sun, moon, or host of heaven was to be stoned to death (Deut. 17:2-5), sun worship prevailed among God's chosen people again and again.

The nations surrounding Israel worshiped many gods. The sun, the most prominent and powerful agent in nature, was worshiped throughout the nations of the ancient world. The Arabians appeared to have paid direct homage to it without the intervention of any statue or symbol (Job 31:26-28). In Egypt the sun was worshiped under the title of Ra. Baal of the Phoenicians, Molech of the Ammonites, Hadad of the Syrians, and Bel of the Babylonians, were also deities of the sun.

Not only were the Israelites forbidden to substitute the works of creation for the creator, and this included men and angels (Rev. 22:8,9), but they were not permitted to make an image or likeness of God for an object of worship. This is the purpose of the second commandment.

Many people today who may not bow down to idols, nevertheless, find their worship is not acceptable because they have permitted other objects to rob God of the love and affection that rightly belong to him. One writer named nine gods which people worship: gold, fashion, fame, ease, intellect, travel, chance, passion, and drink. When any of these or other things dominate a life, they are as other gods, and when they occupy the mind during the worship of God, the worshiper is not *fully* occupied with God.

Christ

Because Jesus is God, he accepts worship (Matt. 14:33; 28:17; John 9:38). When men sought to worship Peter, Paul, and Barnabas, they became angry (cf. Acts 10:25,26; 14:11-15). Compare their reaction with the Lord's acceptance of worship (cf. Matt. 14:33; Luke 5:8; 24:52; John 20:28). Peter and Thomas openly testified to Christ's deity (Matt. 16:16; John 20:28,29). And Christ, because he is God, accepted these testimonies. Christ said, "all men should honor the Son, even as they honor the Father" (John 5:23; cf. 10:30). This implies a demand for worship.

ACCEPTABLE Worship

Heb 9:7,14

Rom 8:7,8

Rom 8:26,27

John 4:24

1 John 3:18

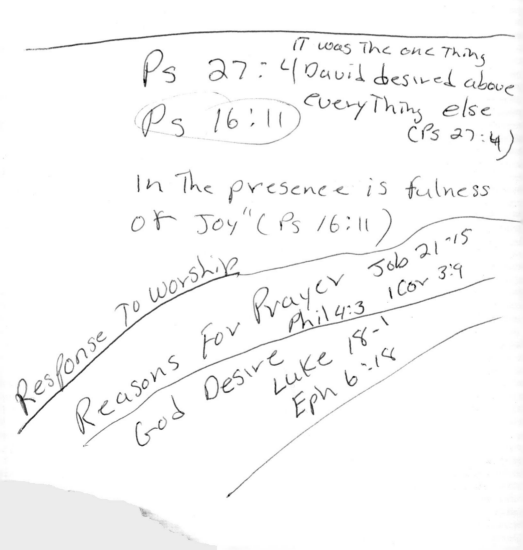

Ps 27:4   IT was The one Thing David desired above everyThing else (Ps 27:4)

Ps 16:11

"In The presence is fulness of Joy" (Ps 16:11)

Response To Worship

Reasons For Prayer   Job 21-15

Phil 4:3   1 Cor 3:9

God Desire

Luke 18-1

Eph 6:18

CARDONE Industries, Inc. • 5670 Rising Sun Avenue • Philadelphia, PA 19120-2595
Telephone: 215.912.3000 • Facsimile: 215.912.3469 • Web Site: www.cardone.com

Paul in his epistles makes it plain that "at the name of Jesus every knee should bow, of things in heaven, and things in earth, and things under the earth and every tongue confess that He is Lord" (Phil. 2:10).

ACCEPTABLE WORSHIP

God is the omnipotent, omniscient, omnipresent one, and the believer's worship must be pleasing to him, *never* taken lightly or done carelessly. In order for worship to be acceptable it must be in the name of Christ, guided by the Holy Spirit, and in conformity with the Word of God.

The Christian can pray to and worship God directly only because of Christ's death and resurrection (Heb. 9:7,14). The veil of the temple which shut out all but the high priest from the Holy of Holies, or the most holy place, was torn from top to bottom at the crucifixion of the Lord. Christ opened the way into the most holy presence of God, so that the believer may now enter and worship.

True worship, which is acceptable to God, is that which the Spirit inspires. "They that are in the flesh cannot please God" (Rom. 8:7,8). God is seeking worshipers who worship in the Spirit and have "no confidence in the flesh." To please God in worship, the Christian must turn his eyes from himself and ask the Holy Spirit to teach him and to "help his infirmities" (Rom. 8:26,27).

God does not accept a pretended worship. It is possible to bow the head and even the body without bowing the soul in reverence before God. The true worshiper approaches God with a desire to glorify him and enjoy him. He comes without showiness and pride, but with sincerity and an offering of gratitude and prayer (John 4:24; I John 3:18).

RESPONSE TO WORSHIP

True worship creates response in the worshiper. As the face of Moses shone after his communion with God (Exod. 34:29,30), so the radiance of heaven will be manifest in the life of the true worshiper. In fact, there is no higher, deeper, nor purer joy than that which springs from the adoring contemplation of God. Such joy fills the soul as the Christian bows in worship, occupied and satisfied with God. It was the one thing David desired above everything else (Ps. 27:4) and prompted him to write, "In thy presence is fulness of joy" (Ps. 16:11).

41

PRAYER

The reading of God's Word and prayer occupy an important place in a service of worship. When a believer reads the Bible, God is speaking to him, when he prays, he talks to God. God has provided his Word; his child must read and study it to hear his voice. He has provided prayer; his child must communicate with him through prayer to understand and apply his Word.

REASONS FOR PRAYER

From one of the oldest books in the Bible comes the question, "What profit should we have, if we pray unto him?" (Job 21:15). God can work without the believer's prayers, and often does, but He prefers to have the Christian cooperate with Him in carrying out His plans. "We are laborers together with God," true yoke-fellows, fellow laborers (I Cor. 3:9; Phil. 4:3).

There are many reasons why believers pray.

God's Desire (Luke 18:1; Eph. 6:18)

God wants the believer to be in constant fellowship with him. Any situation and any request can be brought to him at any time. God promises, "If ye shall ask any thing in my name, I will do it," (John 14:14). God works as the believer prays. Through prayers God moves the hearts of men, breaks down barriers, reveals pathways, supplies needs. Both the assurances in God's Word and the evidences of answered prayer guarantee his desire for and use of prayers.

Believers' Needs and Desires (Ps. 40:17; Heb. 4:16; I Pet. 5:7)

Only God can supply all the believers' needs. He gives exceeding abundantly above all that the believer asks or thinks (Eph. 3:20). Individual needs are not the only reason for the Christian to pray. The harvest is great, the laborers few; therefore, he prays for the needs of the whole world (Luke 10:2). All men need to be saved; therefore, he prays for all men (I Tim. 2:1-4). The church of Christ needs continual support; therefore, he prays for all believers (Eph. 6:18). Only God can fulfill desires. Where there is delight in God's will, he will give the desires of the heart (Ps. 37:4).

Spiritual Power (Matt. 6:13; 26:41)

"The spirit indeed is willing, but the flesh is weak." The Christian is continually tempted by the world, the enemy around him; the flesh, the enemy in him; the devil, the enemy beside him. Many evil desires cannot be overcome in one's own strength. But God has provided prayer through which the Christian communicates with him and receives strength to withstand temptation.

Satan's Defeat (Eph. 6:11,12; James 4:7,8)

Prayer is not only a calling on God, but a conflict with Satan. To resist Satan's attacks, the believer must draw closer to God in prayer.

REQUIREMENTS FOR PRAYER
Aware of a Relationship to God (I John 1:9)

The privilege of prayer is only for those who know Christ as their Savior and have the awareness that their sins are forgiven. But even the child of God may have his prayers hindered because of unconfessed sin (Ps. 66:18). If so, he has the blessed privilege of confessing that sin to him who is faithful and just to forgive him and cleanse him from all unrighteousness. Prayer enables the believer to see what is wrong; prayer adjusts the soul.

It is not always some flagrant sin that prevents real communion with God. More often, it is little hindrances that mar fellowship with God and make prayer ineffectual. It is the "little foxes," says Solomon, that "spoil the vines" (Song of Sol. 2:15).

There must be perfect union between the Lord and his child. The true Christian abides in and obeys him. Answer to prayer is conditioned on the believer's obedience. He must not knowingly disobey the revealed will of God, but actively strive to carry out Christ's commands.

With Right Attitude (Jer. 29:13; James 5:16b)

It is the effectual, fervent prayer that avails much. To pray with "all the heart" is to put forth all spiritual energy in prayer, remembering that the devil would prevent the answers to prayers if possible. Charles Finney said, "Prevailing, or effectual, prayer attains the blessing that it seeks. It is that prayer that effectually moves God. The very idea of effectual prayer is that it affects its object."

"Praying Hyde," the missionary whose prayer life stirred all India, found that the obstacle preventing a prayer being answered was the lack of praise. He would then confess this as a sin, and ask for forgiveness and for the spirit of praise. As he praised God for souls, the souls always came. Along with telling God needs and desires, the Christian must not neglect to praise and thank Him.

Without Ceasing (I Thess. 5:17; Rom. 12:12)

It is as possible to "pray without ceasing" as it is to breathe without ceasing.

The soul needs stated times of prayer each day. This "quiet time" fills the soul with spiritual power and blessing, leading to a continual spirit of prayer and fellowship with God. The Christian's ability to stay with God in his quiet time measures his ability to walk with God at all other times.

The word for "ejaculatory" prayer comes from *jaculum,* a dart or arrow, and fittingly describes prayer which "darts" up to God at any time. The short, emergency prayers owe their point and efficiency to the longer prayers that have preceded them. Thus prayer is both an act and an attitude.

According to God's Will (I John 5:14)

All prayer is based on God's revelation of himself and his will. His promises encourage and his commands motivate the believer to pray, but his will sets the necessary limit of prayer. The believer asks in faith lest he be like a tossing wave (Heb. 11:6; James 1:6); he prays in submission to God's will lest he ask amiss (James 4:3). A will wholly yielded to God is able to say, "Not my will, but Thine by done."

Prayer in fleshly strength will affect fleshly results, "for whatsoever is born of the flesh is flesh." God is the only giver of life. The highest function of the believer is to be a transmitter of the life of God to others. This is accomplished through prayer. Prayer connects one with the source of life and power.

RESPONSIBILITY TO PRAY

For the Christian to "cease to pray" is sin (I Sam. 12:23). God has made him responsible for bringing things to pass through prayer. He who has great gaps in his prayer life will have no "sense of grip" in prayer. God would have him bring "into captivity every thought to the obedience of Christ" (II Cor. 10:5). Some will say, "What a price to pay!" But consider what such a price purchases!

SUMMARY

Worship means to concentrate on God, to think about his power and majesty. It is a spiritual act, and the need to worship can only be fulfilled when the believer worships God as he has commanded. Objects or people must never take his place. Christ, as God, accepts worship and one day the entire universe will rec-

ognize him as Lord and bow before him.

The Christian should not worship carelessly. True worship is in the name of Christ, guided by the Holy Spirit, and conformed to God's Word. It creates a response of pure joy because the worshiper is satisfied and occupied with God alone.

When the Christian reads the Bible, God speaks to him. When he prays, he talks to God. Prayer is vital for the believer. God desires prayer and works through it; the believer expresses his needs and desires in prayer; spiritual power is received, and Satan is defeated by prayer.

The Christian must allow God's Holy Spirit to direct him when he prays. Unconfessed sin will hinder prayers, so the believer must confess sins and be conscious of forgiveness. In striving to serve Christ, the believer is in union with him—abiding and obeying. This abiding calls for continual prayer. In addition to stated times of prayer in which the soul is filled with spiritual power, the Christian must be in communication constantly. Effective prayers are made with all the heart, filled with praise and thanks, and spoken in accordance with God's will.

For the Christian, it is a sin not to pray. Prayer is a responsibility and a blessing from God.

DISCUSSION QUESTIONS

1. What is true worship?
2. Why do you think many people are careless in worship?
3. What three things are required to make our worship acceptable and why?
4. How does the Holy Spirit guide in worship?
5. How are God's Word and prayer related?
6. Explain how our prayers are hindered.
7. How can the Christian pray without ceasing?
8. Why should praise and thanksgiving be included in prayer?
9. Since God knows all our needs before we ask him, why should we pray?
10. What is the relationship of true worship and prayer?

RESOURCES

Gibbs, Alfred P. *Worship, the Christian's Highest Occupation.* Kansas City, KS: Walterick Publishers, n.d.

Lavender, John Allan. *Why Prayers are Unanswered.* Wheaton, IL: Tyndale House, 1981.

Origin and Purpose of the Church

The English word *church* is a translation of the Greek word *ecclesia*. It means "the called-out." The members of the church are called out from the old creation into the new (II Cor. 5:17). Though they are in the world, they are not of the world. The Father has given them to the Son out of the world (John 17:6, 11, 14, 16). They are Christ's body of believers.

The church is more than an organization, it is an organism. An organization is a body of persons enlisted together for united action. An organism is a body having life within itself, with mutually dependent parts, all functioning toward a common purpose. This purpose for the church is the spread of the gospel to all men.

The church has a record of service through the ages. The way in which it has expanded, from its small beginnings in a remote Roman province into a great world institution, gives it an historical perspective unequaled by any international organization. Medieval history largely centered around the church, which was the great factor in the civilization of Europe. Modern history centers on international and interracial relations and has followed in the wake of the world-wide missionary movement of the church. The church is responsible for the founding of many benevolent services including orphanages, homes for senior citizens, and youth programs. The education of the masses began with the church. True, these movements have not all maintained their original Christian standards, but they were started by men of God and have been used by God for good.

ORIGIN OF THE CHURCH

The church is a New Testament institution which had its birth with the outpouring of the Holy Spirit at Pentecost, but its conception was long before that.

ORIGINATED WITH GOD

The church originated in the mind of God and is an important part of his program for the earth. The importance of the church is recognized by the fact that its program was determined and its members chosen "before the foundation of the world" (Eph. 1:4). There is no room here for chance or uncertainty. God's plans are complete and his purposes definite.

God the Father is the author of the salvation which the church proclaims. Christians can do nothing to earn God's grace. Their possession of "all spiritual blessings in heavenly places" is not because of what they have done. God himself chose the members of the church, predestined them to be conformed to the image of his Son, and accepted them in Christ. (Eph. 1:3-6).

The members of the church are redeemed by the Son of God. The death and resurrection of Christ provide access to God and show God's plan to unite the entire universe in Christ (Eph. 1:7-11).

But God's record concerning Christ cannot be believed without trusting in him. Faith comes by hearing the truth of the gospel, and God honors the faith of the members of the church by sealing them with his Holy Spirit. "In whom also after that ye believed, ye were sealed with that holy Spirit of promise, which is the earnest of our inheritance" (Eph. 1:13,14).

ANNOUNCED BY CHRIST

The first mention of the church in the New Testament is in Matthew 16:16-18, but no supremacy was here given to Peter, for a comparison of these verses with other Scriptures (Matt. 18:15-20; John 20:19-23) clearly reveals that the same privilege of binding and loosing was given to other disciples, and to the whole church. The rock upon which the church was to be built was the

Lord Jesus Christ who is the "chief corner stone" (Eph. 2:20). "Other foundation can no man lay than that is laid, which is Jesus Christ" (I Cor. 3:11).

FOUNDING OF THE CHURCH

The church had its first converts on the day of Pentecost (Acts 2). Pentecost was known as the Feast of Weeks, and the Jewish law required the attendance of all males at the celebration in the temple (Exod. 23:14-17; 34:22). Jerusalem was the central gathering place for the Jews, not only those of Palestine, but also those from the whole Roman Empire. This explains the presence of the vast multitudes, and especially the people from other lands. Although born and brought up in other countries, the Jews remained faithful to their laws and in strict observance of them; consequently, thousands had come to Jerusalem for this feast. These Jews heard the apostles speak in the language of those countries from which they had come. As representatives from foreign lands, they were in reality the first missionaries of the church whose members Christ commissioned to preach the gospel "unto the uttermost part of the earth" (Acts 1:8).

The men and women who became the first members of the church all came from the Jewish faith. They were, however, divided into three classes: Hebrews, Hellenists, and Proselytes.

The Hebrews were those whose ancestors had lived in Palestine. In their synagogues they read the Hebrew Scriptures faithfully, and interpreted them sentence by sentence into Aramaic which was the common language.

The Hellenists were Grecian Jews whose homes, if not ancestry, were in foreign lands. After their conquest of the Orient by Alexander the Great, Greek became the leading language of the world, and on this account Jews of foreign ancestry were called Grecians, or Hellenists. They represented the most intelligent and most prosperous branch of the Jewish people.

Proselytes were Gentiles who had accepted the Jewish faith. Although a minority among Jewish people they were to be found in many synagogues in the Roman Empire.

PURPOSE OF THE CHURCH

The world is filled with a variety of nations and languages, but God divides all into three great groups of people—Israel, the Gentiles, and the church (I Cor. 10:32). Israel had three main purposes in God's redemptive plan. Israel was to be: entrusted with the Scriptures (God's Word); a channel to introduce the world's Redeemer; a witness to the world.

The study of the Old Testament reveals that while Israel realized the first two purposes for which the nation was set apart, she failed in the third. The New Testament introduces the church, whose members were commissioned as *witnesses* of God's plan of salvation, to both Jews and Gentiles. But that is not the only mission with which the church has been entrusted.

A REVEALED MYSTERY

The word "mystery" is found twenty-seven times in the New Testament, with about one-half of these referring to the church. In the New Testament this term means a revealed secret, or a divine truth once hidden but now disclosed. "According to the revelation of the mystery which was kept secret since the world began, but now is made manifest" (Rom. 16:25,26).

The church was "hid in God" from the beginning of the world. Not even the angels or the prophets knew of the "church" or its vital part in God's plan.

What had been concealed from angels and prophets was revealed to Paul to record. The mystery "hid in God" was the divine purpose to make of Jew and Gentile a new creation, the body of Christ, formed by the baptism of the Holy Spirit in which the earthly distinction of Jew and Gentile would disappear (I Cor. 12:12,13; Col. 3:10,11).

That the Gentiles were to be saved was no mystery. Those who had the Old Testament realized that Christ was to come for the salvation of both Jew and Gentile. This was plainly foretold (Isa. 42:6; 49:6; Rom. 9:24-33). But never had there been such a marvelous announcement as this: "Christ in you, the hope of glory" (Col. 1:27). The unfolded mystery was that Christ should gather out a people, live *in* them, and work *through* them.

THE BODY OF CHRIST

The church had its beginning at Pentecost when the believers were all assembled, according to divine directions (Acts 1:4). Christ was at the right hand of God, but he sent the Holy Spirit to dwell in each believer. The Holy Spirit united the believers to Christ and also to one another, and thus the body, the church, was born (Rom. 12:4,5; I Cor. 12:12-27).

This body of Christ has been formed "to the praise of the glory of his grace, wherein he hath made us accepted in the beloved" (Eph. 1:6). Christ as the head is united by the closest spiritual ties with the members of his body. One spirit of love unites them in complete fellowship. Christ is not only Lord over us, but he also is dwelling *in* us as members of his body. The relation between Christ and the church is not to be that of king and subject, but one of husband and wife, a relationship of perfect intimacy and spiritual union. We have been called to the *fellowship* of God's Son (Eph. 3:14-19; Col. 1:12-18).

This body of Christ has work to do on earth. Certain officers are to be chosen by the church "for the perfecting of the saints, for the work of the ministry, for the edifying of the body of Christ" (Eph. 4:12). The object of this general ministry on the part of every member is the building up of the body of Christ, the increase of its membership, the completing of it as an organism (Eph. 4:15,16).

THE BRIDE OF CHRIST

The membership of the church must be completed before the Son of Man can come in his glory (Rev. 19:7; II Cor. 11:2). Christians labor for the completion of the church, for when this object is gained the Lord will return. The bridegroom will have his bride, which will be presented and united to him.

The church will be with Christ in heaven, for God has "made us to sit together in heavenly places in Christ Jesus: that in the ages to come he might show the exceeding riches of his grace in his kindness toward us through Christ Jesus" (Eph. 2:6,7). The union between Christ and his church is divine and will continue eternally.

SUMMARY

The word "church" means "the called-out." The members of the church are called *out of* the world to be Christ's body and his messengers *in* the world.

Originating in the mind of God, the church was determined before the foundation of the world. God the Father originated the plan; God the Son died for the salvation of believers; and God the Holy Spirit sealed believers and revealed truth. Hence, all three persons of the Trinity took part in the birth and growth of the church. Christ himself announced the first church.

The church was born on the day of Pentecost. Jews from all over the Roman Empire were gathered in Jerusalem for the Feast of Weeks and, on that day, the Holy Spirit spoke through the small group of believers in the languages of the many foreigners. The Jews that were converted went back to their homelands to spread the news. Three major groups became members of the first church: *Hebrews*—Jews in Palestine who spoke Aramaic; *Hellenists*—Jews of foreign ancestry and who lived in other lands; *Proselytes*—Gentile converts to the Jewish faith.

At last called into existence to witness of God's salvation, the church had been a mystery, a secret "hid in God" from the world's beginning. Neither the angels nor the prophets knew of the divine plan to draw both Jews and Gentiles together into one body with Christ as the head. In addition, the Holy Spirit would dwell in all believers, uniting them with God and with one another.

When the membership of the church is completed. Christ will unite the church with himself, as the bride to the bridegroom. Believers will be with him in heaven, glorifying him eternally.

DISCUSSION QUESTIONS

1. Explain the meaning of the word "church."
2. What is the origin of the church?
3. According to Matthew 16:18 what was the rock on which Christ said he would build his church?
4. Why were so many nations represented in Jerusalem at Pentecost?
5. Describe the three classes that were members of the first church.
6. Why was the church called into existence?
7. What is meant by the word "mystery" in the New Testament?
8. Explain the mystery of the church as it was revealed to Paul.
9. Describe the church as "the body of Christ."
10. Describe the church as "the bride of Christ."

RESOURCES

Beyer, Douglas, *Basic Beliefs of Christians.* Valley Forge, PA: Judson Press, 1981. Chapter 9.

Demaray, Donald E. *Basic Beliefs.* Grand Rapids: Baker Book House, 1958. Chapter 8.

Dowley, Tim, (ed). *Eerdmans' Handbook to the History of Christianity.* Grand Rapids: Wm. B. Eerdmans Pub. Co., 1977.

Shelley, Bruce L. *What is the Church? God's People.* Wheaton, IL: Victor Books, 1983.

Growth, Character, and Organization of the Church

GROWTH OF THE CHURCH

The Christian church was founded on the day of Pentecost (Acts 2:1 ff), when the Holy Spirit moved in a wonderful way in the hearts of men. The marvelous events that followed and that form the account of the earliest history of the church are, in reality, the acts of the Holy Spirit (Acts 4:31; 5:32; 13:2; 16:6).

MESSAGE

The church held three fundamental beliefs:

Jesus Is Messiah (Acts 2:36; 5:31; 17:3)

All the disciples gave witness that Jesus of Nazareth was the long expected Messiah of Israel who died, rose again, and is exalted at God's right hand. Each member of the church was expected to give personal loyalty, reverence, and obedience to him as Savior.

Jesus Rose from the Dead (Acts 4:33; 13:33; 17:31)

The resurrection was proclaimed not only as proof of Christ's deity, but also as evidence that God had accepted his atonement for sin and appointed him to judge the world in righteousness.

Jesus Will Return (Acts 1:11; 15:16)

The disciples believed and taught that Jesus had ascended to heaven and was to come back to earth and reign. This blessed hope supported the believers in the midst of great need, danger, and persecution.

METHOD (Acts 1:8,22; 5:32; 10:39; 13:31)

The method of the church through which the world was to be won was the witnessing of its members. As the numbers were multiplied, the witnesses multiplied, for every member felt his responsiblity for actively furthering the work. This universal testimony was a powerful influence in the rapid increase of the church.

However, the building process is not merely the addition of numbers. The early church also built up its members by teaching them in a continual program of Christian education. The disciples literally obeyed the Lord's great commission to go and teach. The word "teach" is found twice in our Lord's farewell address, and the instruction in teaching was, "to observe all things whatsoever I have commanded you."

MOVEMENT (Acts 4:4; 5:14; 6:7; 9:31; 11:21; 14:1; 16:5; 17:4)

There were daily additions to the number of believers, and only a short time after the day of Pentecost the number reached five thousand. At the end of the first century, Pliny told the Emperor Trojan that "so many believe in Christ that the temples of pagan worship are deserted." At the end of the third century there were no less than five million believers. By the tenth century there were fifty million members and at the opening of the nineteenth century approximately two hundred million professed Christ.

The classic history of ancient Rome is given by Gibbon in *Decline and Fall of the Roman Empire,* written in the eighteenth century by a scholar who was distinctly antagonistic to Christianity. Gibbon named four distinct reasons why Christianity grew so rapidly in the ancient world:

Enthusiasm

The Christians believed and applied the teachings of Jesus, and refused to compromise with any pagan religion or secular code.

Doctrine of Future Life

Christians have a hope of future glory that cannot be understood by human intellect. The early Christians held this hope and shared it with certainty.

Miraculous Power

"With great power gave the apostles witness" (Acts 4:33). Marvelous miracles worked by the disciples demonstrated the truth of their teaching.

Pure Morals

They would not compromise with pagan immoralities. They abandoned sins when they became Christians, lived exemplary lives, and exhibited a standard of virtue unknown to the ancient world. The early Christians exhibited what Paul calls, "the mystery of godliness." Their aim was to be like Christ in all areas of life.

CHARACTERISTICS OF THE CHURCH

Today there are vast differences in the characteristics of an average church. In every local assembly there may be both saved and unsaved members. The characteristics of any local church are the total of the characteristics of its members. The early Christians were:

UNITED (Acts 2:44; 4:32; Eph. 4:1-7)

"All that believed were together, and had all things common." The Christians united not only as a church, but also as a family. Many Jewish converts were ostracized by their families and friends, so the Christians helped and encouraged one another. Their mutual faith in the Messiah bound them together as a group. And the Holy Spirit worked mightily as a result of their unity.

STEADFAST (Acts 2:42; Eph. 4:14-16)

Their *doctrine* did not turn aside from facts to fables. They remained steadfast in their belief in God's Word and the apostles' teaching.

They recognized their vital need for *fellowship* and remained steadfast in it. If the members had stopped to criticize, no doubt they would have found faults in each other. Instead, they were quick to see their own failures, but slow to criticize others.

Christ was the substance of sermons and the center of worship. The institution of the *Lord's supper* and of *baptism* represented the work of grace in the hearts of the early believers and they remained steadfast in observing these.

The believers continued steadfast in *prayer,* praying "with one accord," together, in agreement (Acts 1:14). The early church realized the power in prayer and God's faithfulness to answer.

CHARITABLE (Acts 2:45; 4:34,35; Eph. 4:28)

They "sold their possessions and goods, and parted them to all men, as every man had need." The members gave spontaneously. Their love for Christ and their desire to spread the gospel were so great that they saw their material possessions as gifts *from* God to be used *for* him. Their sharing came as the result of Christian affection and faith, not by legislated direction or force. Their charity was a wonderful testimony of the love of Christ in their lives. Those who looked on the scene could well comment, "See how those Christians love."

JOYFUL (Acts 2:46,47; Eph. 5:18-21)

They continued "daily with one accord in the temple . . . with gladness and singleness of heart." It was this singleness of heart that gave them joy. They were not divided between Christ and the world, but being wholly the Lord's, they rejoiced in the Lord and were full of his joy.

SUCCESSFUL (Acts 2:41,47; 5:14; 6:7; 13:44; 16:5; 17:6; 18:8)

For the first two centuries the church spread like a wild-fire of such vast proportions that the whole world was "turned upside down."

The early church had *favor with God* and its members were added to the Lord and by the Lord. Frequently today only the names of members are added to churches. These names increase the numbers, but not the churches' strength. When the Lord adds to the church, the members are united, steadfast, charitable, joyful. As a result, their presence makes the church successful.

It is remarkable that in spite of opposition and persecution from rulers and governments, the early church also had *favor with men.* The sincerity and joy of these first Christians could not fail to impress the men of the world.

ORGANIZATION OF THE CHURCH

That there were organized churches in the first century is clear from the fact that Paul addressed many of his epistles to groups in different localities. The first letter to the church at Corinth shows that certain forms of service were recognized (I Cor. 12:4-11). Paul's later epistles to Timothy and Titus contain directions for a well-organized congregation of believers. Local administration by recognized officers, and the presence of the Council at Jerusalem (Acts 15), indicate an established order in the developing church.

OFFICERS

In the beginning of the church, there was no clergy. This and other offices were created as the need arose. Just as kings, judges, and generals came into existence to meet the needs of civil society, so the clergy developed to meet the needs and responsibilities of the growing church.

Elders (Acts 11:29,30; 14:23; 20:17; I Tim. 5:17; Titus 1:5)

While the institution of the office of elder is not definitely stated in Scripture, it was so well known and understood that it is believed to have been the familiar mode of governing the Jewish synagogues (Matt. 15:2; 21:23; 26:57), which in turn grew out of the organization of Israel (Exod. 19:7; 24:1; Josh. 23:2). The name originally suggested advanced years, but came to signify the office for which one was especially fitted by wisdom and maturity of age. A similar honor was conferred by the Romans on their senators, or old men, who composed their governing body. That the officers of the early church bore this familiar title is in itself suggestive of the fact that they performed the well-known duties of rule and government.

The apostles were called elders (I Pet. 5:1), but as their number was limited to those who had seen the Lord Jesus after his resurrection (Acts 1:21,22), they soon passed off the scene. Hence their leadership was temporal.

The elders were also called bishops or overseers (Titus 1:5,7). The former was a name more familiar to the Jewish convert, but the latter to the Gentile, to whom it suggested government, for the term was already common under Roman rule.

The elders were often designated pastors (Eph. 4:11) to emphasize the fact that they were the divinely appointed shepherds who were to "feed the flock of God." They were, therefore, the appointed teachers and spiritual guides in the early Christian church.

Deacons (Acts 6:1-6; Phil. 1:1; 1 Tim. 3:8)

The office of deacon began with the appointment of Philip and Stephen and their five fellow-laborers. The office was primarily created to relieve the apostles of various menial tasks in order that they might give themselves wholly to prayer and to the ministry of the Word. The duties of deacons did not include preaching and teaching, nevertheless they were among the first preachers of the gospel (Acts 6:8-10; 8:5). In like manner they were the first evangelists, because their specific duties sent them to the homes of the poor. They constructed the framework of the institutions of charity in the church. In comparison with the number of elders, the deacons were few, but this magnified rather than minimized their office.

QUALIFICATIONS

Great care was exercised in the selection of elders. The qualifications for this important office are listed in I Timothy 3:1-7. The elder was to be blameless and of good reputation. He was to prove his capacity for governing the church by first showing his ability to rule his own home. Furthermore, he was to be sober, discreet in mind, orderly in conduct, hospitable, and able to teach. He was not to be quarrelsome, greedy, or a recent convert that could be blinded by pride.

Similarly, I Timothy 3:8-13 describes the qualifications for deacons. The deacon, like the elder, was to be a husband of one wife (who herself was to be serious, truthful, sober, and faithful in all things), a father known to be capable of managing his children and of ruling well his own house. As he was to be selected from the younger men, he was to serve first on probation, and when fully approved, appointed to his office.

RESPONSIBILITIES

In the early church there was no distinction between elders, bishops, and pastors as there is today. Even the office of deacon was not always limited to the care of the poor, but frequently included the responsibilities assigned to the elders, as in the case of Stephen and Philip. However, the responsibilities administered by these officers were divided into three distinctive tasks:

Evangelizing

The evangelist planted the church. He was the missionary and extension worker. The apostles served in this capacity. Paul, the

57

only apostle of whose work we have detailed account, travelled from one place to another. His chief object was "to preach the gospel, not where Christ was named" (Rom. 15:20), and his epistles suggest a long list of churches that he planted.

Shepherding

The pastor shepherded or governed the church. He was ordained in every church that the apostles founded, and carried on the work the evangelist had begun. This work included supervising, preaching, and visiting.

Christ summed up *supervising* when he spoke of assigning "to every man his work" (Mark 13:34) and the task to "each according to his own ability" (Matt. 25:15 NAS). The unparalleled success of the early church was due largely to the fact that every member was an active participant. The apostles realized that Christ established the church for the development of workmen as much as for the accomplishment of work (Eph. 2:10).

Paul speaks of *preaching* in II Timothy 4:2 and Titus 2:1. Timothy was the pastor of the church at Ephesus, and Titus of the church at Crete. In Paul's epistles to these two young men there is much concerning their pastoral duties, especially the content of their preaching.

Visiting church members, especially when they were in sickness or in sorrow, was a particular duty of the pastor. As the shepherd of the flock, he was to minister to the weak and the helpless, the poor and the needy.

Teaching

The teacher edified, or built up, the church. Teaching was more common than preaching in the early church. While John the Baptist was a preacher, Christ was a teacher. Sixty out of ninety times that Jesus was addressed, he was called teacher. And he commissioned his followers to teach as well as to preach (Matt. 28:19,20). While the words for "preaching" are found about 150 times in Scripture, those for "teaching" are mentioned about 250 times. The early church saw the vital importance of continually teaching its members from the Word of God.

SUMMARY

The Christian church was formed on the day of Pentecost and the Holy Spirit has acted in its continued spread and growth.

Holding three fundamental beliefs—that Jesus is Messiah, rose again, and will return—the church grew in numbers by witnessing and the members grew from the continual teaching they received.

Christianity spread rapidly. Gibbon suggests four main reasons: enthusiasm, doctrine of the future life, miraculous power, and pure morals. The believers were united, steadfast, charitable, joyful, and successful. These factors stood out in sharp contrast to the paganism surrounding the church.

After its birth at Pentecost, the church soon became well organized. Offices were created as the need arose to meet the responsibilities of the growing church.

The office of *elder* may have grown from a similar office in the Jewish synagogues, and perhaps from the senators within the Roman government. It suggested the wisdom and maturity of advanced years. The apostles were called elders. Bishops, overseers, and pastors were other names for this office.

Deacons took over various menial tasks to allow the apostles to concentrate on prayer and the ministry of the Word. Stephen and Philip, two of the first deacons, were preachers as well as evangelists. This office formed the framework for the institutions of charity in the church.

Qualifications for each office are described in I Timothy 3. Their duties included evangelizing, shepherding, and teaching.

DISCUSSION QUESTIONS
1. Describe the three fundamental beliefs of the early church.
2. Describe the two methods of growth in the early church.
3. Why did Christianity spread so rapidly?
4. Explain the importance of the five characteristics of the early church.
5. In light of these characteristics, compare the early church with the church today.
6. Distinguish between the elders and deacons.
7. Why did Paul write so specifically concerning qualifications?
8. Describe the three major duties of the church officers.

RESOURCES
Shelley, Bruce L. *What is the Church? God's People.* Wheaton, IL: Victor Books, 1983.

Werning, Waldo J. *Vision and Strategy for Church Growth.* Grand Rapids: Baker Book House, 1983.

Angels

The Bible contains many passages about angels. Yet there is a tragic and widespread ignorance, even among Christians, concerning the Bible doctrine of angels. Because of this ignorance, distorted pictures and varied superstitions have corrupted the doctrine concerning these spirit beings. The Bible has much to say about the origin, nature, and ministry of angels.

CREATION OF ANGELS

Angels have not always existed. They had a beginning. They were created by a divine command (Neh. 9:6; Col. 1:16).

NUMBER AND RANK (Job 25:3; Matt. 26:53; I Thess. 4:16; Heb. 12:22; I Pet. 3:22; Rev. 5:11)

Such expressions as "ten thousand times ten thousands," "a multitude of the heavenly hosts," and "myriads of angels," suggest that their numbers are beyond human calculation if not comprehension.

There are various grades or ranks of angels, having different positions and capacities. Although God created them similar enough to recognize their divine origin, he manifested variety among these beings. Angels are called powers, archangels, seraphim, cherubim, and celestial armies of the Most High.

SUPERIOR TO HUMANS (Ps. 8:4,5; II Kings 19:35; Acts 5:19; Luke 20:36)

Humans were created lower than the angels. Angels are invisible and immortal, and moreover are not as people confined to this earth. Angels are spirits created apart from their habitations. God gave heaven to the angels for a home, but "the earth hath he given to the children of men." Further contrasts will be observed between the character of the angels and that of humans.

SUBORDINATE TO GOD (Eph. 1:20,21; Col. 2:18; Heb. 1:6-8,13; Rev. 19:10; 22:8,9)

Great as may be their superiority to humans, angels are vastly inferior to God. The theme of Hebrews chapter one is the superiority of Jesus Christ to angels. He "became flesh, and dwelt among us," and thus became "a little lower than the angels." Yet when he returned to heaven he was set at the right hand of God, "far above all principality, and power, and might, and dominion."

Angels never permitted people to worship them. One of the principal reasons for the writing of the Epistle to the Colossians was to correct the prevailing practice of angel worship which some of the early Christians had taken over from the pagans—a practice which proves that the ancient world believed in angel worship.

CHARACTERISTICS OF ANGELS

HOLY (Matt. 25:31; Luke 9:26; Acts 10:22; Rev. 14:10)

Angels in their unfallen state are completely pure. They are in a state of established and superior holiness, and are not tempted with evil. Their refusal to receive worship from humans is evidence of this. Their whole nature abhors that which is evil. Their moral perfection is shown by such phrases as "holy angels" and "the elect angels."

Angels are glorious beings. Only a few places is their appearance to people accompanied by a description of their personality. It is interesting to note that Christ, in speaking of his return, refers to the glory of the angels as well as to his own (Luke 9:26).

INTELLIGENT (II Sam. 14:20; I Cor. 13:1; Gal. 1:8)

Both Old and New Testaments contain high estimates of the wisdom of angels. The scholarly Paul acknowledged their superior intelligence. However, they are not omniscient, as is God. We read that the church was just as much a mystery to the angels as to the Old Testament prophets (I Pet. 1:12), and that the hour of the Lord's return is unknown to them, as it is to us (Mark 13:32).

MIGHTY AND POWERFUL (Ps. 103:20; II Thess. 1:7)

Not only do they "excel in strength," but also they are spoken of as "mighty." In Revelation, angels are attributed with carrying out various judgments which affected millions of people. However, while mighty, they are not almighty, and are in subjection to God (I Pet. 3:22).

Undoubtedly angels can move more swiftly than light (186,000 miles per second). Perhaps they move as rapidly as thought. Daniel was told that at the beginning of his prayer the angel Gabriel was commissioned to fly swiftly that he might be with him at the close.

HUMBLE AND OBEDIENT (Isa. 6:2; II Pet. 2:11; Jude 9)

The seraphim Isaiah saw were a high order of angels, but they humbly covered their faces in the presence of the Lord. Michael, an archangel, when contending with an angel of greater authority, showed humility by calling on God to rebuke him.

The fact that the Lord taught his disciples to pray, that his will be done on earth as it is in heaven, indicates that all in heaven are obedient. And this obedience is prompted by love. Because the holy angels love God, they obey him.

MINISTRY OF ANGELS

Angels are perfect in character. Every angel renders consecrated service of praise to God (Ps. 148:2). Angels are at the same time both worshipers of God and servants of men (Heb. 1:14). The Lord set forth this truth when he said that the angels of children ever behold the face of the Father in heaven (Matt. 18:10).

GUIDANCE (Luke 2:10-12; Acts 8:26; 10:3,7,8)

Angels sometimes appeared to God's people to announce his plan for their lives, or to direct the work he had for them to do. It is of particular interest to note that angels are deeply interested in the Christian's work. In the cases of Peter and Cornelius, an angel guided the Christian worker to the sinner and the sinner to the Christian worker. Angels watch over the relationships of believers with non-believers. They rejoice each time a sinner repents and returns to God (Luke 15:10).

COMFORT (Matt. 4:11; Luke 22:43)

The angels' ministry of comfort is evident in the lives of Hagar, Elijah, and Paul: *Hagar* when she first fled from Sarai (Gen. 16:7,8); *Elijah* when he ran away into the wilderness to escape Jezebel's wrath (I Kings 19:2-8); *Paul* when he was shipwrecked (Acts 27:23,24).

Spurgeon said: "It is my firm belief that angels are often employed by God to throw into the hearts of his people comforting thoughts. Angels came and ministered unto Jesus, and I doubt not that they minister unto us. Few of us have enough belief in the existence of angels."

PROTECTION (Ps. 91:11; Isa. 63:9)

Angels fulfill a protective ministry over God's people. Angels are also shown as protectors of the nation of Israel (Exod. 14:19; 23:20) and of Daniel (Dan. 6:22).

These portions of Scripture indicate God's great love. What greater blessing can the believer receive than the protection from danger by God's angels?

DELIVERANCE (Ps. 34:7)

Several times it was evident that angels delivered the apostles from persecution during their ministry.

When the Jews imprisoned Peter and some of the other apostles, an angel came by night, opened the jail doors, and led them out (Acts 5:17-19).

Later, when Herod imprisoned Peter intending to kill him, an angel appeared in his cell, woke him, broke his chains, and freed him (Acts 12:6-9).

Prison walls, iron gates, and the guard of four soldiers could not prevent angels from rescuing the seemingly doomed apostles.

JUDGMENT (II Thess. 1:7-9)

Several accounts in the Bible tell of the angels' ministry of judgment.

In Genesis 19, God's judgment on wicked Sodom and Gomorrah was executed by two angels.

David had a choice of three penalties for his sinful pride in numbering the people to estimate the strength of his armies. In choosing plague rather than famine or defeat, he threw himself on the mercy of God and of the angel that executed the decree (II Sam. 24:15,16).

The Assyrian army seemed unconquerable. City after city had fallen before the victorious armies of that rising world power. Jerusalem appeared doomed. But that night when the city was in despair, Hezekiah prayed, and an angel slew 185,000 of the enemy (II Kings 19:35).

CORRUPTION OF ANGELS

The study of the holy and righteous character of God makes it impossible to believe that he would have created anything that was essentially and originally evil. The study of mankind shows that he was created perfect, but by an act of willful disobedience he corrupted his nature and became sinful. The same is true of the fallen angels. They were not created thus. Peter says that they sinned (II Pet. 2:4), while Jude declares that they "did not keep their positions of authority but abandoned their own home" (Jude 6 NIV).

It is not easy to discover all of God's dealings with these majestic creatures with whom he has surrounded himself as partakers of his holiness and participants of his glory. From widely scattered implications however, the events that might have taken place can be pieced together.

THE ANOINTED CHERUB (Ezek. 28:14)

"Cherub" was the highest rank in the angelic world. A study of the word "cherubim" (plural of cherub) as presented in Scripture (Ezek. 1:5-14; 10:8-22; Rev. 4:6-11; 5:11-14) intimates that this superior rank of God's creatures sat nearest to God's throne and led the worship of the entire universe. The use of the word "anointed" here, would indicate that Lucifer was the chief of the cherubim, a position to which he was especially appointed by God.

REBELLION

Scripture tells the cause of Lucifer's unrest, dissatisfaction, and final rebellion. The glory of his position and the magnificence of his person were more than he could bear. Pride ruled his heart and overwhelmed him (I Tim. 3:6). His heart was lifted up because of his beauty, and his wisdom was corrupted by reason of his brightness. Like Absalom, the handsome son of David (II Sam. 15:3-6), he sought by stealing the hearts of the unstable in the kingdom, to occupy the seat of royalty.

How graphically Isaiah describes the ambition of this haughty monarch, Lucifer! For while he refers to the king of Babylon, he also describes the powerful and prosperous Lucifer who aspired to be God (Isa. 14:12-15; cf. Acts 12:21-23).

When Lucifer imagined that he might be God, rebellion ruled his heart, and he plotted against Him to whom he had formerly been loyal and obedient. Then, doubtless, dissatisfaction appeared among the angels, which only strengthened him in defiance and disobedience.

DEFEAT

Lucifer's rebellion was unsuccessful, as God foreknew. The result of this conflict between heavenly forces was defeat for Satan and his followers. They "prevailed not; neither was their place found any more in heaven" (Rev. 12:8). The results of that overthrow were Satan's loss of position and the creation of a successor to fill the vacated place in heaven.

The rebels of heaven were dealt with speedily and severely. "God spared not the angels that sinned, but cast them down to hell" (II Pet. 2:4). Though they were very great and very powerful, God did not spare them for that. Even their vast numbers made no difference. There was no delay. Punishment followed hard upon the crime (Isa. 14:15; Ezek. 28:17).

Since pride was the cause of the first terrible misdeed that marred the holiness and happiness of heaven, God in his omniscience formulated a penalty in just proportion to the transgression. The sin of pride was punished by an exhibition of grace. A subordinate race was created and placed on the earth. God saw fit to "ordain strength" out of far weaker and lowlier creatures (Gen. 1:26-28; Ps. 8:2-5).

SUMMARY

The subject of angels is not well-known even among Christians. As a result, many misconceptions and superstitions have distorted this doctrine. But the Bible has much to say about angels.

Angels are created beings. They have various ranks and are referred to in Scripture by many words. Angels are superior to humans yet subordinate to God.

The Bible has much to say about the characteristics of angels. They are: holy, intelligent, mighty and powerful, humble and obedient.

Angels have a varied ministry and purpose. They carry on a ministry of guidance, comfort, protection, deliverance, and judgment.

Angels, like humans, were created perfect and also, like humans, by an act of willful disobedience became corrupt. The Bible says that Lucifer, the chief of the angels, rebelled against God and sought to be God. Lucifer (then called Satan) was unsuccessful, lost his position of authority, was punished and thrown out of heaven.

DISCUSSION QUESTIONS

1. Why is there such widespread ignorance about angels?
2. What does the Bible tell us about the number and rank of the angels?
3. Give references showing angels' position in relation to mankind and to God.
4. Name the characteristics of the angels.
5. When and where did angels serve in the ministry of guidance?
6. Name some Bible characters that were protected by angels.
7. List some occasions when angels have ministered deliverance.
8. What led to Lucifer's rebellion and defeat?
9. What happened as a result of Satan's defeat?
10. Discuss the position and service of angels since Bible times.

RESOURCES

Beyer, Douglas. *Basic Beliefs of Christians.* Valley Forge, PA: Judson Press, 1981. Chapter 6.

Dickason, C. Fred. *Angels: Elect and Evil.* Chicago: Moody Press, 1975.

Ryrie, Charles C. *A Survey of Bible Doctrine.* Chicago: Moody Press, 1972. Chapter 5.

Character, Work, and Worship of Satan

9

Satan has already been conquered by Christ's death and resurrection, however he is still present as ruler of this world. Previous chapters treated Satan's former position as God's anointed angel, his fall, and his temptation of the first humans. The character of Satan, his further work on earth, and the reality that he is worshiped will now be considered.

THE CHARACTER OF SATAN

Multiple Scripture passages leave no doubt as to the true nature of Satan. In the Old Testament he is called "Belial," which means lawlessness, and indicates that his character is completely evil. In the New Testament he is called "Beelzebub" the ruler of evil spirits and "Apollyon" the destroyer. The name "Satan" means adversary; "devil" means slanderer.

WICKED

The Lord taught his disciples to ask deliverance from the "evil one" (Matt. 6:13 NIV). Christ also calls him "the evil one" in the parable of the sower (Matt. 13:19). Satan is a murderer and a liar from the beginning (John 8:44). He stirred up the firstborn son of human parents to slay his brother, and he has been active ever since in multiplying every kind of evil (I John 3:8,12). He will do everything in his power to mar the righteousness of the believer and to intensify the wickedness of the sinner.

POWERFUL

The glimpses of Satan in Scripture reveal his "power and signs and lying wonders" (II Thess. 2:9). By his power the unbeliever is blinded and in darkness (Acts 26:18). Only faith in Christ can give light and forgiveness of sin. By Satan's power the believer is hindered in service (I Thess. 2:18). Only by resisting him and drawing nigh to God can the believer have victory (James 4:7,8a).

Satan has power over a kingdom and rules exalted beings called principalities, powers, world rulers, spiritual hosts of wickedness (Eph. 2:2; 6:11,12). He is called the "great red dragon" (Rev. 12:3) to symbolize his terrible character, as well as his awesome power.

SCHEMING

Satan is a schemer. He will take advantage of any opportunity and has a plan of attack for all conditions and all circumstances. After Jesus spent forty days in the wilderness, Satan came to tempt him through his physical weakness (Matt. 4:2,3). At the height of Jesus' popularity, Satan again tried to tempt him through the crowd's desire to crown him king (John 6:15). People's weaknesses are prime targets; Satan emphasizes these weaknesses and attempts to use them for evil. Strengths and successes can also be subtly colored to meet Satan's ends. The devil is never more dangerous than when he pretends to be an "angel of light" (II Cor. 11:14), deceiving people with what *seems* good, pure, and right. He will attack the mature believer as well as the new Christian. All Christians must be constantly aware of Satan's craftiness and be watchful so he can never have the advantage (II Cor. 2:11).

THE WORK OF SATAN

TEMPTATION

Satan's activities illustrate his character. The book of Job shows something of what he is doing on earth. In Job, chapters 1 and 2, the angels appear before God to give an account of their work. Satan is among them. On being questioned, he declares that he has been making a careful investigation of men and matters on the earth. God calls his attention to Job as "a perfect and an upright man," and asks Satan if he can find anything with which to accuse Job. Satan challenges God to let him test Job's loyalty, and God grants his request.

First, Satan is permitted to destroy Job's family and property with armies, lightning, and a whirlwind. Still Job remains faithful. A second conference is held in heaven, and again God calls attention to Job's loyalty despite Satan's afflictions. To this Satan replies that God did not permit him to go far enough. If God will only give him permission to afflict Job's body in addition to his other calamities, Satan is sure that Job will curse God. Satan is permitted to tempt him further, but "in all this did not Job sin with his lips" (2:10).

However, Satan does not always tempt men by affliction. He knows people will turn from God if they are tempted to love the world. According to I John 2:15,16, "all that is in the world" includes the lust of the flesh, the lust of the eyes, and the pride of life.

Satan appeals to the carnal nature in men, urging them to gratify their sensual desires at any cost. He would have all believe that self-gratification and pleasure are the goals for life.

Those who have too much self-respect to waste their lives filling every sensual desire, Satan tempts with the multitude of things around them. Possessions are often successfully used to turn people from God.

Those who cannot be enticed with pleasure and possessions, Satan puffs up with a sense of their own importance, and a desire to be important. He glorifies fallen humanity, making people believe that the power and reason to live is in themselves. As one theologian has said, "The satanic message for this age is reformation and self-development, while the message of God is regeneration by the power of the Spirit."

DECEPTION

Satan is the prince of liars. He seems to be at his best when he can delude men into denying his existence, or act as the "angel of light" so people cannot see him working. He gets into the pulpit or the theological classroom and pretends to teach Christianity, when in reality he corrupts it! The deceiver presents his lies as truth. The gospel with which Satan deceives men (Gal. 1:6,7) praises the life of Christ but disregards his death. It magnifies him as a teacher

69

but gives no place to his work as Savior. As "god of this world," Satan blinds "the minds of them which believe not, lest the light of the glorious gospel of Christ . . . should shine unto them" (II Cor. 4:4).

In the parable of the sower, it was "while men slept" that Satan sowed the tares (Matt. 13:25-30, 37-40) among the wheat. The tares resemble the wheat, and it is only with difficulty that they can be distinguished. Satan sows his children among the believers in the church, and often they cannot be distinguished. They weaken and defile the church, but God promises judgment (Rev. 12:9).

TORMENT

Satan "as a roaring lion, walketh about seeking whom he may devour" (I Pet. 5:8). No one can escape his anger against the people created to replace his lost standing in heaven (Rev. 12:12).

Satan Authors Sickness and Death (Luke 13:16; Heb. 2:14)

In the final analysis, Satan is responsible for most sickness. The diseases that Jesus healed were brought on people by the devil. It was Christ who delivered the woman whom Satan had tormented with pain for eighteen years. Every separation by death owes its existence to him.

Satan Provokes Persecution (Rev. 2:10)

Satan stirred up the Jews, and later the Greeks and Romans, to persecute the early church. He prompted the tyrant Nero to destroy Christians. He invented the inquisition chamber and the cruel tortures of the Reformation.

Satan Causes Believers to Deny Christ (Luke 22:31,61,62)

Peter wept bitterly after Satan had caused him to deny his Lord.

THE WORSHIP OF SATAN

It seems impossible that people can be found in conscious worship of Satan. Yet it is possible there are on earth today more worshipers of Satan than worshipers of God.

Idolatry is not merely the worship of wood or stone, it is in reality the worship of Satan, and the Bible warns against sacrificing "unto devils, not to God" (Deut. 32:17). Those who submit themselves to evil spirits have "changed the truth of God into a lie, and worshiped and served the creature more than the Creator" (Rom. 1:25). We need to proclaim the truth that "they may recover themselves out of the snare of the devil, who are taken captive by him at his will" (II Tim. 2:26).

DEMONISM

The worship of demons and their possession of human beings existed not only before Christ came (Lev. 17:7; Ps. 106:37) but also after his sacrificial death.

Distinction should be made between the words "devil" and "demon" or "spirit." In revised versions of the New Testament "devil" always refers to Satan, the one "devil," the leader, or head, of a host of demons. A person is not possessed by the devil, but by spirits or demons. While powerful, Satan is neither omnipotent nor omnipresent; but he works through many demons. In matters of gravest importance, Satan himself probably appears. This was notably the case in the temptation of Christ.

Christ Cast Out Demons

The gospel writers record at least six miracles in which the Lord cast out demons.

The unclean spirit (Mark 1:23-26; Luke 4:33-37)
The demon in one blind and dumb (Matt. 12:22)
A legion of demons (Mark 5:1-20; Luke 8:26-39)
The demon in a dumb man (Matt. 9:32,33; Luke 11:14)
The demon in a girl (Matt. 15:22-28; Mark 7:24-30)
The demon in a boy (Matt. 17:14-21; Mark 9:14-29)

That these were not cases of insanity or epilepsy is proved by the demons' superhuman strength and knowledge, recognizing Jesus as God's Son, and securing permission to dwell in animals. The demons, not the persons possessed, speak to Christ; Christ speaks to the demons, and not to the persons possessed.

The Apostles Cast Out Demons

Christ commissioned his disciples to cast out demons (Matt. 10:8 NAS; Mark 16:17 NAS). The early church leaders encountered demon-possession in many of the places they taught.

Peter, at Jerusalem (Acts 5:14-16)
Paul, at Philippi (Acts 16:12-18)
Paul, at Ephesus (Acts 19:11-17)

In addition to the above instances, demon-possession was encountered in Samaria and Paphos, which would suggest that it was a rather common experience. These demons manifested superhuman knowledge and power, but the apostles always possessed superior ability through the Holy Spirit (I John 4:4).

SPIRITISM

Spiritism is the belief that the spirits of the dead can communicate with and present themselves to people. It is generally supposed that they do this through the agency of a human being called a "medium." The spirits of the dead do not revive; it is demons that assume bodily forms to deceive those who would communicate with the dead.

The Bible speaks strongly concerning spiritism.

Expressly Forbidden (Lev. 19:31; Isa. 8:19; Micah 5:12)

The Bible condemns spiritism. Witchcraft and soothsaying were recognized as terrible realities and given a character which is completely evil. The entire practice is condemned.

Death Penalty Decreed (Exod. 22:18; Lev. 20:27)

God fixed the death penalty for those involved with evil spirits. God's command to Joshua to destroy the Canaanites (Deut. 18:9-14) was the execution of a righteous sentence of God upon a wicked people. Israel became the executioners that they might be warned "not to learn to do after the abominations of those nations," lest they suffer a similar fate.

These abominations are listed as divination, enchantment, sorcery, consulting with familiar spirits, witchcraft, and necromancy (spiritism). Doubtless the Canaanites were adulterers, thieves, and murderers, but it was their involvement with evil spirits that brought the final destruction.

After Samuel died and Saul had ruthlessly murdered the priests of Israel, there was no one to whom he could go for information. He ordered his servants to find him a woman possessed of a familiar spirit whom he might consult concerning the outcome of the fatal war he was waging with the Philistines. A medium was found at Endor. Being requested to call up Samuel, she began her preparations. But God overruled the satanic powers and the real Samuel appeared instead of the anticipated personification. The unhappy king committed suicide, not only for his bloody crimes, but for "asking counsel of one that had a familiar spirit, to inquire of it" (I Chron. 10:13,14; I Sam. 28:3-20).

ASTROLOGY

Astrology believes that the stars influence human lives. Astrologers need no telescope, spectroscope, micrometer, or multiplication tables to determine human destinies. A fertile imagination and a gullible public are all the equipment they need.

The accuracy of the predictions of God's prophets as compared with those of the astrologers is seen in that marvelous challenge of Isaiah to Babylon just before he revealed the name of Cyrus, its future conqueror: "Let now the astrologers, the stargazers, the monthly prognosticators, stand up, and save thee from these things that shall come upon thee" (Isa. 47:12,13).

Daniel's contest with the astrologers of Babylon is also familiar. Nebuchadnezzar revealed the shallowness of the horoscopes of his day by insisting that the "wise men" reveal the forgotten dream as well as give the interpretation of it. Listen to his estimate of these men: "If ye will not make known unto me the dream, . . . ye have prepared lying and corrupt words to speak before me" (Dan. 2:9). The astrologers considered such a demand to be absurd, and though their lives were at stake, they had to admit the limitation of their art and profession which the nations had been led to hold in such high esteem. The true status of the astrologer, past and present, was revealed by the remarkable reply that Daniel made to Nebuchadnezzar: "The secret which the king hath demanded cannot the wise men, the astrologers, the magicians, the soothsayers, show unto the king; but there is a God in heaven that revealeth secrets, and maketh known to the king Nebuchadnezzar what shall be in the latter days" (Dan. 2:27,28).

Astrology today, as in former times, is linked with Satan and offers his predictions of the future as a substitute for faith in a heavenly Father. God "frustrateth the tokens of the liars, and maketh diviners mad" (Isa. 44:25).

SUMMARY

Although Satan has been conquered, he is still the ruler of this earth. His character is completely evil. He stirs up every kind of wickedness; he blinds the unbeliever and hinders the service of the believer. As a ruler, he exercises awesome power. Through his scheming he is able to use all circumstances, good and bad, for his own purposes. Using peoples' strengths as well as their weaknesses is another deceitful tactic. He is especially dangerous when he appears as an "angel of light."

As a tempter, Satan used affliction as well as "the lust of the flesh, the lust of the eyes, and the pride of life" to draw people away from God. He makes people love the world and all that is in it. He is a deceiver, presenting his lies as the truth, forming a gospel that disregards Christ's work as Savior. By sowing "tares" among the "wheat," he weakens the church. He is also a tormentor causing: sickness and death; persecution; believers' denial of Christ.

There are many people who worship Satan. Idolatry, demonism, spiritism, and astrology are all examples of involvement with evil spirits, and all are forbidden by God. Christians need to proclaim the truth against the lies of Satan.

DISCUSSION QUESTIONS

1. What do the Bible titles for Satan reveal about his character?
2. Explain three additional characteristics of Satan.
3. How is Satan's scheming illustrated in the Scriptures?
4. What can be learned about Satan's work from the book of Job?
5. What three appeals are used in all temptations?
6. In what respect is Satan a deceiver?
7. Describe four ways in which Satan is revealed as a tormentor.
8. Explain how idolatry is Satan-worship.
9. What distinctions should be made between devil and demon (or spirit)?
10. How do we know that the demon-possessed people in the gospels were not cases of insanity or epilepsy?
11. What is the teaching of Scripture regarding spiritism?
12. What is the Christian position on the use of astrology?
13. Discuss the relationship of Satan's activities to current world events.

RESOURCES

Beyer, Douglas. *Basic Beliefs of Christians*. Valley Forge, PA: Judson Press, 1981. Chapter 6.

Bubeck, Mark I. *The Adversary*. Chicago: Moody Press, 1975.

Dickason, C. Fred. *Angels: Elect and Evil*. Chicago: Moody Press, 1975.

Sanders, J. Oswald. *Satan Is No Myth*. Chicago: Moody Press, 1983.

Resurrection and Judgment

The resurrection is an assured fact. Careful examination of God's Word provides overwhelming evidence. People cannot deny the resurrection without first disposing of many evidences. These evidences include all four gospels with their concluding chapters on Christ's resurrection, the historic credibility of the book of Acts, and every other piece of writing remaining from the first century that proclaims the resurrection. To deny all these evidences would be to deny Christianity itself. The resurrection of Christ is the foundation of Christianity. To deny the resurrection is to deny history and to deny truth.

RESURRECTION OF BELIEVERS

The resurrection and eternal life are precious promises. Those whose names are written in the book of life have these promises (Dan. 12:1; Rev. 21:27).

FOR THE CHILDREN OF GOD

The Sadducees were the liberals of Christ's day. To their way of thinking, religion for this life was the important thing. Heaven was a vague place, and all thoughts of future existence were but idle dreams. When they asked Jesus a question concerning marriage in the resurrection, they thought they had asked him an unanswerable question (Matt. 22:23-33). They hoped that he would either deny the resurrection, or would make some statement which would contradict the law of Moses on the matter of the marriage of a relative's widow. But as usual Christ replied wisely. The amazing wisdom of his answer completely silenced them. But what is most interesting is his statement about a special resurrection of the believer. "But they which shall be accounted worthy to obtain that world, and the *resurrection from the dead*, neither marry, not are given in marriage: neither can they die any more; for they are equal unto the angels; and are the children of God, being the *children of the resurrection*" (Luke 20:35,36).

FOR THE JUST

In the parable in Luke 14:12-14, Christ is addressing believers. The men and women of this world would entertain their friends with the full expectation that they would have the favor returned on another day. But God's children should give of their substance to those who are not able to repay. Why? Because "thou shalt be blessed; for they cannot recompense thee: for thou shalt be recompensed at the resurrection of the just" (Luke 14:14). If the worldly people would be included on this occasion, there would be no need to distinguish this as "the resurrection of the just." The words "of the just" are superfluous in the passage unless they refer to a distinct resurrection.

BELIEVERS' HOPE

Paul relinquished everything for Jesus Christ (Phil 3:5-8). He was a great scholar, occupied a very high position, and had many friends among the exclusive and influential sect of the Pharisees to which he belonged. But all these honors meant nothing to him after he met Christ, and thereafter his one desire was that he might experience the fellowship of Christ's sufferings and the power of Christ's resurrection. As he expressed it, his one hope was that he "might attain unto the resurrection of (from among) the dead" (Phil 3:11). The resurrection Paul desired could not have been a general resurrection of good and bad. One could experience that, no matter how he lived. It was to be a resurrection of which only those who have known Christ will be participants.

BELIEVERS' CONSOLATION

The familiar passage from I Thessalonians 4:13-18 is often heard at funerals. It was Paul's comfort to Christians who had lost loved ones. Among the disciples in Thessalonica were many who joyfully anticipated an early return of the Lord. As the weeks and months passed and some of their number died without seeing Christ and partaking of the glory of his return, these Thessalonians were troubled lest their loved ones who had died should not share in the joy and glory of Christ's appearing. Paul therefore comforted them with the assurance that those who are alive at the coming of the Lord will have no advantage over the Christian dead. But notice that, whereas he speaks of Christian believers, living and dead, mingling together in joyous fellowship with the Lord, nothing is said about unbelievers. It is evident that those who are not Christ's will not rise with believers at his coming.

ORDER OF RESURRECTIONS

There is much vital instruction in the resurrection chapter of I Corinthians 15, which is one of the longest in the New Testament. Perhaps the most interesting information found here is the order of future occurrences. The schedule of events, beginning with the resurrection of Jesus Christ, is given as follows:

The resurrection of Christ (v. 23)
The resurrection of the believers (v. 23)
The reign of Christ (v. 25)
The destruction of death (v. 26)
The completion of Christ's reign (v. 24)

James M. Gray, former president of Moody Bible Institute, said:

The resurrection of Christ insures that of all men (vv. 20-22); for both the wicked and the good, the unbelieving and the believing, shall be raised, some to everlasting life, and some to everlasting shame and contempt (see also John 5:28,29). But they will not be raised all at once. Christ is the first fruits, whose resurrection has already taken place. The second installment of the resurrection will consist of true believers, who will come forth at His second advent. The third and last will consist of the rest of the dead, who will come forth after the millennium and at the end of the world.

Revelation 20:4-6 not only confirms I Corinthians 15, but is much more explicit in details and time. The expression, "a (or the) thousand years," is used six times in the first seven verses of Revelation 20, and it must be interpreted literally. It is important to note that the reign of Christ is preceded by the *first resurrection,* and that those who participate in it are *happy and holy.* Moreover, the rest of the dead "lived not again until the thousand years were finished" (v. 5).

RESURRECTION OF UNBELIEVERS

There are only two classes of people in relation to the resurrection. On the one hand are those who are absorbed in the pursuit of wealth, pleasure, or other material gains, and know nothing higher than the things of this life.

On the other hand, there are those who believe in the coming of the Son of God and do all in their power to be ready for him. They also must work for a living on this earth, but the things of Christ's church are more important, and their primary purpose is to complete its ministry on earth.

These two classes of people cannot be distinguished easily, but on the days of resurrection there will be no question as to their identity. Those who have "done good" because of personal faith in Jesus Christ as their Savior will come forth in the first resurrection, and those who have "done evil," at a second resurrection (John 5:29).

The passage in Revelation 20:5 states that the unbelievers—the rest of the dead—"lived not again until the thousand years were finished." There are other characteristics that mark the second resurrection.

JUDGMENT   (Dan. 12:2; John 5:28,29; Rev. 20:13)

These passages all relate to the resurrection of the unbeliever which is connected with the great white throne judgment. This judgment takes place at the close, and not at the beginning, of Christ's reign on earth. This resurrection might never have been mentioned in Scripture were it not that this reference is needed to explain the presence of the sinners before the judgment seat of God.

PUNISHMENT (Rev. 20:15)

The resurrection referred to in Revelation 20:15 is associated with punishment. Of necessity, therefore, the participants will be unbelievers.

JUDGMENTS OF BELIEVERS

Most people think of all judgment taking place after the resurrections. One judgment at least takes place before death. "It is appointed unto men once to die, but after this the judgment: so Christ was once offered to bear the sins of many; and unto them that look for him shall he appear the second time without sin unto salvation" (Heb. 9:27,28). Death is decreed on every person because of sin, and sin must be judged. The judgment of believers as sinners has already taken place through Christ's redemptive work on the cross (John 3:18; 5:24).

JUDGMENT AT THE CROSS (John 5:24; 12:31,47,48; Acts 13:39; Rom. 8:1; II Cor. 5:21; Gal. 3:13; I Pet. 2:24)

Judgment in a criminal case is the settlement of a breach against the law of society. Judgment in a civil case is the settlement of a controversy between two individuals. But no one is tried before a judge for guilt if he has already pleaded guilty.

Christ has been appointed to judge the world, and at His judgment the sinner will be on trial for his sins. But if the sinner has previously pleaded guilty and accepted the pardon offered him in Jesus Christ, according to the Bible "there is now no judgment to them which are in Christ Jesus," for by Christ "all that believe are justified from all things, from which (they) could not be justified by the law of Moses." As soon as men plead guilty and accept God's gracious provision for their sins, Christ will answer for them. There is no future judgment of sin for the believer. That has taken place at the cross. Peace and pardon begin right here on earth, and the future can only decree, "He which is filthy, let him be filthy still: and he that is righteous, let him be righteous still" (Rev. 22:11). Our future life is but a continuation of our present attitude toward sin and righteousness.

JUDGMENT AND REWARDS (I Cor. 3:9-15; 4:5; II Cor. 5:10)

These passages in Corinthians have to do solely with believers. Nothing is said about the wicked in these three chapters, so it is conclusive that Paul is speaking about Christians appearing before the judgment seat of Christ. However, this is not a judgment for sin, but for works. Judgment for sin was already accomplished for the believer by Christ. Salvation is a gift. Rewards are earned. This is a judgment of one's accomplishments. The Christian is Christ's "workmanship created . . . unto good works."

All believers build on Christ as their foundation, but some put "gold, silver and precious stones" into the superstructure, and others add nothing better than "wood, hay, stubble." This judgment will test the believer's work by fire. The wise and worthy builder will receive a reward. The unwise builder, although building on Christ as a foundation the same as the other, "shall suffer loss, but he himself shall be saved; yet so as by fire" (I Cor. 3:15).

As men are pardoned individually, so they are rewarded one by one. The result of individual acceptance of God's pardon is eternal salvation, but the result of individual service is the inheritance of the personal treasure laid up where neither moth nor rust doth corrupt, and where thieves do not break through and steal.

Paul spoke frequently about the crowns to be awarded on this day of judgment. He pictured a scene in the Olympic games where there were many runners, though only one secured the prize. But, as Paul has said, it is different with this race. Believers run not uncertainly, for God will reward not only the winner, but all who run according to their ability. Moveover, the reward is not a fading wreath, but an incorruptible crown (I Cor. 9:23-27).

JUDGMENTS OF UNBELIEVERS

The first two judgments concern the pardon and reward of the righteous, the last two have to do with the judgment of the wicked. It is certain that the wicked will die and rise again, and appear at the great white throne judgment. As the first judgment of believers took place during their lifetime, it is interesting to note that the first judgment of unbelievers likewise takes place before death.

JUDGMENT OF THE LIVING NATIONS (Matt. 25: 31-46)

How often this is spoken of as the general judgment, supposed to take place in heaven, at the end of the world! But Matthew 25 does not so indicate. Note that in chapter 24 Christ was talking about his return, and chapter 25 marks the events associated with his return. First, there is the marriage supper of the Lamb (vv. 1-13); second, there is the judgment of the saints (vv. 14-30); third, the judgment of the living nations (vv. 31-46).

This judgment of the nations will be after the judgment of rewards and will take place at the coming of Christ to earth with his saints (Jude 14,15). During the interval between the judgment of rewards and the return of Christ to judge the earth, will occur the world's greatest tribulation, as set forth in Revelation 6-19.

Joel writes that Christ will set up his judgment seat in the Valley of Jehosaphat, that is, Palestine. Thus this judgment will take place on earth (Joel 3:11,12; Zeph. 3:8). This is most reasonable as well as significant inasmuch as Palestine is recognized as the historic, geographic, and religious center of the world, and the Jews for some time have been returning there in great numbers.

This is not a general judgment of good and bad, for there are three classes mentioned—the third being the brethren (Matt. 25:32,40). "My brethren" cannot refer to the church, which has already been translated and rewarded. Neither can they be part of the nations that have been gathered for judgment. In Balaam's prophecy it says that Israel "shall not be reckoned among the nations" (Num. 23:9). It is evident, then, that the "brethren" are Jews who have been converted and have accepted the commission to preach the gospel of the kingdom after the church has been removed from the earth.

The subject of this judgment in Matthew 25 is the relation of the nations to Christian Jews during the tribulation. The wicked nations left on the earth will persecute and fight against the Jews, and Christ, at his coming with his angels and saints, will call the nations into judgment for their treatment of the Jews. Those who have treated them badly will be separated and sentenced to eternal punishment. Those who have favored the Jews—who for the most part will be God's ministers and missionaries (Isa. 66:18,19)—will join in the millennial reign of righteousness. They will form Christ's kingdom on earth, and the saints, both Jew and Gentile, will reign with him.

JUDGMENT AT THE GREAT WHITE THRONE (Rev. 20:11-15)

Note the differences between the judgment of the nations, just described, and this final judgment. The former takes place at the *beginning* of Christ's thousand year reign on earth, the latter at the close. The former deals with the *living*, the latter with the *dead*. There is no resurrection in the former; there is in the latter. The former takes place on *earth*; and the latter in *heaven*. The former deals with conduct toward the brethren; the latter with works recorded in the books.

After Christ has reigned in triumph a thousand years on earth and has put down every enemy, his sovereignty will not be supreme until all who have rejected him as Savior have been brought to trial. For this purpose the wicked of all the centuries will be raised from the dead and brought before him. At some time in their lives on earth each one was confronted with the same question that troubled Pilate, "What shall I do then with Jesus which is called Christ?" (Matt. 27:22). But these unbelievers would not plead guilty of sin. They would not accept the pardon in Christ. Now they will be tried by the Lord. The books will be opened; and for every idle word they shall give an account (Matt. 12:36).

"As I live, saith the Lord, every knee shall bow to me, and every tongue shall confess to God" (Rom. 14:11). Just as surely as there is a living God, the judgment must take place. There can be no stronger language in the Bible than this. He has made the earth and he will judge it.

On that day, "there is nothing covered, that shall not be revealed; and hid, that shall not be known" (Matt. 10:26). People may have deceived their families and friends, but they cannot deceive God. They may have lied to their business associates, but they cannot lie to God.

In that day "every one of us shall give account of himself to God" (Rom. 14:12). Many forget these warning words. They try to blame someone else for their sins. The wicked will be proven guilty with overwhelming evidence against them. They have despised a crucified Savior. They laughed at God's law. But they will not laugh when the books are opened and their guilt is proven. "No sacrifice for sins is left, but only a fearful expectation of judgment and of raging fire that will consume the enemies of God" (Heb. 10:26,27 NIV).

SUMMARY

The Word of God provides assuring evidence of the resurrection. To deny the resurrection, people must first deny all the evidences and prove that they are false.

Believers are called the "children of the resurrection." They are referred to as participating in the resurrection of the just. Paul hoped for and worked toward the resurrection for he knew that there was to be a separate resurrection of believers. Those alive will have no advantage over those who have died before the Lord's return; all will join together. Christ rose first, at a later time believers will rise, Christ will reign, death will be defeated, and Christ's reign will be complete.

Unbelievers will be involved in a second resurrection. At the end of Christ's reign on earth, they will live again for judgment and punishment.

The judgment of believers already occurred at the cross and since believers have acknowledged their guilt and accepted the pardon in Christ, there is not need for judgment. Only works will be judged and rewards given.

At the beginning of Christ's reign on earth, he will judge the living nations according to their treatment of his people, the Jews. A final judgment at the close of his earthly reign will judge all the dead according to their works. Everything will be revealed and each person will receive God's judgment.

DISCUSSION QUESTIONS

1. What overwhelming evidence makes the resurrection an assured fact?
2. What was significant about Paul's hope of a resurrection?
3. Write a schedule of events beginning with the resurrection of Christ.
4. When does the resurrection of the unbeliever take place?
5. What is meant by the judgment of the cross?
6. Explain the judgment of rewards.
7. When and where does the judgment of the living nations take place?
8. What is the difference between the judgment of the living nations and the judgment of the great white throne?

RESOURCES

Ryrie, Charles C. *Dispensationalism Today*. Chicago: Moody Press, 1973.

——————. *A Survey of Bible Doctrine*. Chicago: Moody Press, 1972. Chapter 9.

Walvoord, John F. *The Rapture Question*. Grand Rapids: Zondervan Pub. House, 1970.

Rewards of the Righteous

In the Bible the Christian learns that there are great rewards for the faithful believer. In contrast to other beliefs, only the biblical presentations of life after death evidence the high and holy qualities that distinguish a divine revelation. It apparently is not God's plan to reveal fully what he has prepared for his children, but he allows Christians just enough light to meet their needs of hope, comfort, and encouragement. Three witnesses have been permitted to give a glimpse of the glories to come.

Christ was as familiar with the unseen as with the seen. He had all his information firsthand. He "was in the beginning with God. All things were made by him; and without him was not anything made that was made" (John 1:2,3).

Paul was caught up into the highest heaven, and though the Spirit would not permit him to reveal all he saw and heard, such was his experience that he testifies that to depart and be with Christ is far better than to remain in this life (Phil. 1:23).

John was divinely appointed to reveal these things. On the island of Patmos John received a vision of heaven's glory, which, guided by the Spirit, he recorded in the book of Revelation (Rev.1:9-11,19).

GOING TO BE WITH THE LORD

At death believers immediately depart to be with the Lord. What a reward in itself! They shall not enter a dark unknown nor a state of unconsciousness, but they will be "present with the Lord" (II Cor. 5:8).

The eternal, glorified body is given when Christ comes for his own. Then shall all the believers who have "fallen asleep" in Jesus be joined to those who are alive and remain, and together they will meet the Lord in the air, and thus be with him forever (I Thess. 4:15-17). If eternal separation from God is hell's supreme torment, surely eternal union with him is heaven's greatest joy.

ENTERING A NEW HOME

The earthly home is temporary; but all believers shall dwell forever in the house of the Lord. The new home has been especially prepared for believers by the Lord (John 14:1-3). Those who know the Lord will not be strangers or visitors in heaven.

Paul says in his first epistle to the Corinthians (I Cor. 2:9) that only the spirit of God can know the things which God has prepared for his people.

THE HOLY CITY (Rev. 21:1-17)

The glory of man's civilization is his cities, but all these will be destroyed (II Pet. 3:10). The city is not only the product of man's civilization, but it is the seat of his sin. When Abraham left the decadent civilization of Ur to dwell in tents with Isaac and Jacob, "he looked for a city which hath foundations, whose builder and maker is God" (Heb. 11:10). This was the Jerusalem of David's conquest, but also (agreeing to the law of double reference) the heavenly Jerusalem which shall be revealed in the final era.

By Satan's final overthrow and the judgment of the great white throne, the world will be purged of evil inhabitants. A new heaven and a new earth will replace the old. Thus the stage will be set for the appearance of the Holy City. Note some features of this city:

Magnitude

The height will be equal to length and breadth, in that it will be built up like a pyramid (Rev. 21:16,17). The greatness of Nineveh, Babylon, Rome, Paris, London, will be totally eclipsed by the city of God. It will be the center of all creation.

The twelve gates, each with a name of a tribe of Israel, are

85

guarded by angels so that only saints may enter. The twelve foundations of the wall bear the names of the twelve apostles who laid the foundation of the kingdom of the Lamb (Rev. 21:12-21).

Purity

The city itself is pure transparent gold and adorned with every precious stone (Rev. 21:18-21). The whole atmosphere is that of purity, permanency, and radiance. The sun and moon will no longer be necessary. The Holy City will be more dazzling than the light of the sun, or the light of the largest stars. The glory of God will light the city and "the Lamb is the lamp thereof" (Rev. 21:11, 23; 22:5). Christ will always be the one by whom the Father is made known.

Sanctuary

Because the city *is* a sanctuary there is no need of a special one. All the barriers between God and man are broken down, and the Almighty and the Lamb dwell in the midst like a temple (Rev. 21:3, 22). It is Immanu-El, "God with us," in full reality and in the highest, most intimate way.

The temple was the meeting place between God and his people, and was assigned for his honor and glory. But now that the earth has been purged from sin, God will re-enter it and dwell with his people. Instead of the temple there will be the throne. It is a solitary throne; it is an unshared throne; it is an eternal throne. Instead of bringing their offerings to the temple, the kings of the earth will bring their glory and honor to the throne of God.

Inhabitants

Only those whose names are written in the Lamb's book of life will live in the Holy City (Rev. 21:7, 27). The "just" in Old Testament days looked for such a city. No doubt all the saints of the Lord will have their habitation there (Heb. 11:10, 13-16).

THE "PARADISE OF GOD" (Rev. 22:1-5)

The Apostle John describes in Revelation the paradise of God in which the Holy City lies. In it are found the river of the water of life flowing out of the throne, and the tree of life. The curse is removed and man may partake freely of both. Yet he is definitely dependent upon God.

On either side of the banks of this river will be growing the tree of life the leaves of which will be for the preserving of the health of nations. "To him that overcometh will I give to eat of the tree of life, which is in the midst of the paradise of God" (Rev. 2:7).

RECEIVING REWARDS

While it is true that every believer will dwell in this Holy City, all will not possess the same honor, wear the same crowns, or receive the commendation, "Well done." Only those faithful in life and service will receive special rewards.

Christians are adding to their accounts either works that will stand the test and be rewarded, or dross that will burn and leave them empty-handed. Actions in daily life build on the foundation of Christ—either with gold, silver, and precious stones, or with wood, hay, and stubble (I Cor. 3:12-15). Several Scripture references speak of future rewards:

"Verily there is a reward for the righteous" (Ps. 58:11).

"He that reapeth receiveth wages, and gathereth fruit unto life eternal" (John 4:36).

"Knowing that whatsoever good thing any man doeth, the same shall he receive of the Lord" (Eph. 6:8).

"Knowing that of the Lord ye shall receive the reward of the inheritance: for ye serve the Lord Christ" (Col. 3:24).

BASIS OF REWARDS

One cannot work for salvation. "For by grace are ye saved through faith; and that not of yourselves: it is the gift of God: Not of works, lest any man should boast" (Eph. 2:8,9), but after salvation, God promises to reward every good work. There is a difference between the Bible references which deal with *salvation*, the "free gift," and those which speak of *rewards*, which are earned by works. The Apostle Paul did not doubt his salvation when he feared he might be a "castaway" (or disapproved), but he did feel that, though he preached to others, he might be preaching in the energy of the flesh rather than for the glory of God, and so suffer loss of reward (I Cor. 9:26,27).

Christians will be rewarded according to their walk. Notice the words of the Lord, "I know thy works, and charity, and service, and faith, and thy patience, and thy works" (Rev. 2:19). Christians will be rewarded for the way they live as well as for what they do. By walking "worthy of the Lord unto all pleasing, being fruitful in every good work" (Col. 1:10), and adding Christian living to faith in Christ, they shall have that *abundant* entrance into the everlasting kingdom of the Lord and Savior (II Pet. 1:5-11).

Christians will also receive rewards according to their works (I Cor. 3:8, 13-15; Rev. 14:13). "Behold, I come quickly; and my reward is with me, to give every man according as his work shall be" (Rev. 22:12) is the promise of the Son of God. When believers stand before the judgment seat of Christ for the judgment of rewards, they will be rewarded not according to good intentions, holy ambitions, or large promises, but strictly in proportion to their faithfulness in multiplying the talents which they received (Matt. 25:21). "He which soweth sparingly shall reap also sparingly; and he which soweth bountifully shall reap also bountifully" (II Cor. 9:6). One cannot judge what is of true worth in God's eyes, for human eyes are blinded by spectacular service and the perspective can be faulty.

It is possible to do much in the name of Christ or the church that is not done for Christ at all. It is also possible to perform many humble duties and hidden services of love for Christ which the world never sees. A great sermon preached in man's wisdom and oratory, to please a large congregation, may not stand at all in that day before the fire of God, whereas a simple, sincere testimony of Christ's saving power may shine forth as a gem.

CROWNS AS REWARDS
Incorruptible or Victor's Crown (I Cor. 9:25-27)

After the Grecian games were all over, the runners, wrestlers, and successful contestants assembled before the judges' stand, an elevated seat on which the judges sat, and the winners were given a crown of laurel leaves. Although this was a corruptible crown which would soon fade, Paul probably had it in mind when he spoke of the incorruptible victor's crown. A man who would compete in those games would deny his body many indulgences in order to win the race. So, Paul tells us, this incorruptible crown is for those who "keep under their bodies;" that is, who do not yield to fleshly desires. These victors do not permit themselves to be weakened for service by selfish desires, or to be diverted from the Master's work by worldly pleasures.

Crown of Life (James 1:12; Rev. 2:10; Matt. 5:12; Rom. 8:17, 18)

This is sometimes called the martyr's crown and is mentioned in James and Revelation. However, coupled with these two are numerous passages referring to the special reward awaiting those who suffer much for Christ. God had a crown of life for all those who endure persecution. The martyrs of every age, and of the tribulation period especially, are to receive this crown.

Crown of Glory (I Pet. 5:2-4)

This is the elder's or pastor's crown given by the Chief Shepherd when he shall appear. It is for faithful ministry. Much is said in God's Word about true and false shepherds of the flock. The faithful minister points in but one direction—toward the cross. Many ministers today cater to the perishing praise of their audience, or the wealth of their members, or the acknowledgment of the learned rather than seek after God's crown of glory. There are others who are faithful by preaching the infallible Word of God and the message of the shed blood of the Son of God, who are now being bitterly persecuted. But for these faithful shepherds the crown of glory awaits.

Crown of Rejoicing (I Thess. 2:19; cf. Dan. 12:3; Phil. 4:1)

All cannot win the crown of glory, but every Christian may attain to the crown of rejoicing, for this is the soul-winner's crown. Every believer is not called to preach, but everyone is called to sow the precious seed of God's Word and to be constantly seeking to win others to Christ. Great will be our rejoicing in heaven when we see those who have been led to salvation through our testimony and patient teaching of God's Word.

Crown of Righteousness (II Tim. 4:7,8)

This is the crown for those who love his appearing. Why a crown of righteousness for loving and looking for the second coming of the Lord? John answers this in I John 3:2, 3: "Beloved, now are we the sons of God, and it doth not yet appear what we shall be: but we know that, when he shall appear, we shall be like him; for we shall see him as he is. And every man that hath this hope in him purifieth himself, even as he is pure."

SUMMARY

There are many promises in the Bible concerning future rewards for the righteous. Christ, Paul, and John were able to speak of these glories—Christ knew them, Paul and John were given glimpses.

At death, believers go to be with the Lord and will remain with him eternally. The new home with God is indescribable in beauty and specially prepared for believers. It will be a Holy City, unlike the cities on earth. Only those whose names are found in the book of life will be inhabitants. No sanctuary will be needed because God's presence fills the city. The light will be from God and the Lamb, brighter than the sun or any star. The wall and gates are made of jewels. The foundation bears the names of the twelve apostles, each gate the name of a tribe of Israel. Huge in magnitude, its length, breadth, and height will be equal. Purity permeates the city. This city lies in the Paradise of God where the water of life flows, and the tree of life gives leaves for the preserving of the health of nations.

Believers have accepted salvation and all will live in the Holy City, but individual rewards will be given according to each Christian's walk and work. Each day's actions will be burned and purified at this judgment of rewards. Some will burn up and some will remain.

Crowns are the rewards. These will be incorruptible, eternal crowns for those who did not allow selfish desires to hinder service to God. The crown of life is a special reward for martyrs and those who suffered persecution. To faithful pastors and leaders goes the crown of glory. Soul-winners are presented with a crown of rejoicing. The crown of righteousness is especially for those who love and look for his return.

DISCUSSION QUESTIONS
1. What happens to the believer at death?
2. Describe the believer's new home.
3. Characterize the Holy City.
4. Why is there no temple in the Holy City?
5. What assurances does the believer have of rewards in heaven?
6. Upon what basis will these rewards be given?
7. What is meant by the victor's crown?
8. Compare the crown of life with the crown of glory.
9. Why is the crown of glory called the pastor's crown?
10. What is the soul-winner's crown?

RESOURCES
Smith, Wilbur M. *The Biblical Doctrine of Heaven.* Chicago: Moody Press, 1980.

Punishment of the Wicked

Some people believe that hell does not exist. Their idea of the mercy of God would be inconsistent with such a place. They say it is too awful a concept to be true. In the Garden of Eden Satan proposed only a slight change in God's word by inserting "not" into God's command to make it state, "Ye shall *not* surely die" (Gen. 3:4; cf. 2:17). Satan's addition of one small word was accepted and the world was lost.

There are others who do not believe that hell is eternal. They explain that a compassionate God would not punish men forever. This is a great help to the Devil's cause.

Then there are those who believe there is a hell, but cannot agree that anyone is going there. With them, all people are good as soon as they die. All were sincere, all meant well, and all, *they hope,* go to heaven. This is a common delusion. It is easy to understand the feelings of the little girl who asked her mother where all the wicked people were buried, for she found no mention on the gravestones of any but the good.

This is not a pleasant doctrine. It was not pleasant for Moses to stand before Pharaoh and proclaim the overthrow of Egypt, for

Elijah to stand before Ahab and proclaim punishment for Israel's sins, for Jeremiah to predict the downfall of Jerusalem, for Stephen, Peter, nor Paul to preach to their persecutors.

No teacher was more loving than the Savior, and yet no one ever spoke more severely about the punishment of the wicked. Hell and destruction were ever before him. To him the punishment of the wicked was clear and essential and to those who look upon him as their Savior from hell, the divine record he left is full of truth and meaning.

Terrible as it is to think of eternal anguish, it must be true or our tender Lord would not have said it. The same lips that voiced the Beatitudes and told of the many mansions in heaven, referred also to "everlasting fire" and "weeping and wailing and gnashing of teeth." There can be no doubt. Jesus Christ settled the *fact* of the future punishment of the wicked.

PARTICIPANTS OF PUNISHMENT

All those whose names are not found written in the book of life will be punished (Rev. 20:15). These will be raised up at the second resurrection and judged guilty according to their sins. In this vast multitude there will be those whom the Bible calls: children of Satan; hypocrites; unbelievers.

Christ was very particular to point out that Satan has his children in this world. Their chief characteristic is that they do not love righteousness, but are rather the enemies of righteousness. And because Christ's righteousness is not in their hearts, envy, malice, murder, and falsehood rule their lives (Matt. 13:38-42; John 8:44).

No one had more to say about hypocrites than did Christ. He constantly exposed their falseness. Satan is the great deceiver (Rev. 12:9), and those who, like him, pretend to be one thing and are something else, must eventually be punished with him (Matt. 23:13-15; 24:51).

People need not be murderers or hypocrites to find their way to hell. Everyone guilty of sin is under condemnation. Only those whose names are written in the book of life because they believed in the atonement of Jesus Christ will be saved. All unbelievers are damned (Luke 12:46; John 3:18; 8:24).

PURPOSE OF PUNISHMENT

The wicked are said to "die in their sins" (John 8:21). They hang onto their sins to the very last. "Wrath" indicates the settled mind of God toward the persistently wicked (John 3:36); "indignation" is the outburst of that wrath at the day of judgment.

But God is also "long-suffering" and desires to lead sinners to repentance (Rom. 2:4-9). He is "not willing that any should perish, but that all should come to repentance" (II Pet. 3:9). He has no pleasure in the punishment of the wicked (Ezek. 18:23, 32; 33:11). He not only gave man an opportunity in the beginning to live forever, but he provided for man's redemption after he had fallen. What more could he have done as a righteous ruler? A righteous God must punish sin.

PLACE OF PUNISHMENT

"Where is hell?" asked the skeptic. "Anywhere outside of heaven," was the answer. While it is true that to miss heaven is hell, and that eternal torment may well be realizing the truth too late, hell is not "just anywhere."

HELL (SHEOL, HADES) (Job 2:2; I Pet. 5:8; Rev. 20:2, 3, 10)

Satan is not now in hell. Satan is the god of this world, and he and his angels are now very busy on this earth. The word "hell" is "hades," in the Greek and "sheol," in Hebrew. It means the place of departed spirits.

LAKE OF FIRE (GEHENNA) (Matt. 10:28; Rev. 19:20; 20:14)

In very plain and definite words the Lord declared that in the future life people will have bodies, and that the bodies of the lost will remain in a literal, physical place of torment. The word "Gehenna," which Christ used, represents the same place and punishment as the "lake of fire" mentioned in the book of Revelation. "Gehenna" means punishment after death. As it receives both soul and body, it comes into existence, therefore *after* the resurrection.

Gehenna was the name of a valley near Jerusalem where the garbage and refuse of the city were constantly burning. Jesus used it to typify what is elsewhere expressed in Scripture as "everlasting burnings" (Isa. 33:14), "everlasting fire" (Matt. 25:41), unquenchable fire (Mark 9:43; Isa. 66:24), and the lake of fire.

PERIOD OF PUNISHMENT

The words "everlasting" and "forever" are used repeatedly to indicate that the punishment is endless. In fact, the same words that are used to speak of the reward of the righteous are likewise employed to designate the duration of the penalty of the wicked (Dan. 12:2; Matt. 25:46; Jude 13; Rev. 14:11; 19:3; 20:10). The one lasts as long as the other; and it is only if there is an end to the joy of heaven that there will be a termination to the misery of hell.

There are some who change Scripture and seek to comfort themselves in the belief that the use of the word "destruction" means annihilation. But this is destruction of opportunity rather than of existence. How can those who are annihilated be said to be tormented, to weep and wail? How can they be said to plead for admission into heaven, and to reason on the subject (Luke 16:23, 24)?

NATURE OF PUNISHMENT

Spurgeon said, "Can you bear to see a fellow-creature in pain? His agony draws forth our sympathies. But you cannot compare the pains of this life with what is to come."

BANISHMENT (Matt. 13:49, 50; 25:41; Luke 16:26; II Thess. 1:9)

God now confers many blessings upon the wicked. "The rain falleth upon the just and the unjust." But when he once says, "Depart from me, ye workers of iniquity," that will be the last they will see of everything that is good and upright and lovely. There will be no voice of prayer, no hymn of praise in hell. There will be no pursuit of knowledge, no acquisition, no occupation, no relief, no hope. Hell is everything evil and abandoned.

DARKNESS (Matt. 8:12; 22:13; 25:30; Jude 13)

The picture is that of an evening banquet. The wicked are thrust out from the merriment of the dinner party into the darkness and gloom outside. Those who have been in the arctic regions say that an even greater hardship than the severe cold are the months of lingering darkness with accompanying depression. The darkness of hell will be impenetrable and eternal.

FIRE (Mal. 4:1; Matt. 3:12; 13:40, 50; Luke 16:23, 24)

It is an accepted law of language that a figure of speech is less intense than the reality. There is no pain like that of burning. Fire is the most destructive and devouring of all elements. Fire is of all elements most opposed to life. Creatures can live in air, earth, and water, but nothing can live in fire.

But the most terrible characteristic of this fire is that it does not consume those that must dwell in flames. They are tormented in the flame, and the rich man is pictured by the Lord as piteously pleading for one drop of water to cool his parched tongue.

REMORSE (Isa. 66:24; Matt. 8:12; 13:42, 50; 22:13)

What is meant by the phrase, "where the worm dieth not?" This worm is probably memory. When God says, "Son, remember," men will never be able to forget. They will remember their sins. They will everlastingly remember God's mercies. They will never be able to forget that they heard the gospel and neglected the privilege of being saved. It is this which will bring bitter pangs of remorse. There will be perpetual weeping over lost opportunities.

Christ speaks of hell and it seems that people would desire to do everything in their power to escape. But such is not the case. Despite the fact that God has done all he can do to save people from this awful fate, they willfully neglect his salvation. Most vividly did Christ sketch the picture of the rich man in hell pathetically begging that someone be raised from the dead to warn his doomed relatives. But would men listen to someone raised from the dead? Lazarus was raised from the dead. And did the Jews listen to him? No, they sought to kill him. Christ was raised from the dead. And still people did not listen to him or the good news of salvation.

SUMMARY

Many people attempt to deny the existence of hell, to deny that it is eternal or that anyone will go there. But Christ himself spoke often of hell and punishment for the wicked.

Those whose names are not written in the book of life will be punished. These will include the children of Satan who do not love righteousness, hypocrites, and all who do not believe in Christ as Savior. These people must be punished for God is holy and, therefore, he must punish sin.

Satan is now allowed to roam the earth, but one day he will be cast into hell and the lake of fire. The wicked will be punished with Satan forever. This punishment does not mean complete annihilation; but conscious torment. This torment includes banishment from all that is good, impenetrable darkness, fire that does not consume, and remorse over lost opportunities to receive Christ.

DISCUSSION QUESTIONS ·

1. In what way does Satan attempt to conceal the existence of a place of punishment?
2. Describe the participants of punishment.
3. What is the chief characteristic of the children of Satan?
4. What is the real purpose of punishment?
5. Discuss the place of punishment for the wicked.
6. In what respect was Gehenna a symbol of the lake of fire?
7. Describe the four penalties involved in the punishment of the wicked.
8. How does Scripture describe the fire of hell?
9. Explain the punishment of remorse.
10. What has this study meant to you personally?

RESOURCES

Demaray, Donald E. *Basic Beliefs*. Grand Rapids: Baker Book House, 1958. Chapter 14.